EMMANUEL CHABRIER
AND HIS CIRCLE

By the same author:

MODERN MUSIC: ITS AIMS AND TENDENCIES

MUSIC IN THE MODERN WORLD

DEBUSSY

ERIK SATIE

RAVEL: LIFE AND WORKS

INTRODUCTION TO THE MUSIC OF STRAVINSKY

EMMANUEL CHABRIER

AND HIS CIRCLE

ROLLO MYERS

WITH EIGHT PAGES OF PLATES
AND MUSIC EXAMPLES
IN THE TEXT

LONDON
J. M. DENT & SONS LTD

Made in Great Britain
at the
Aldine Press · Letchworth · Herts
for
J. M. DENT & SONS LTD
Aldine House · Bedford Street · London
First published 1969

SBN: 460 03826 5

CONTENTS

NOTE

The Harvard system of bibliography has been used in this book, under which only the name of the author and the date of the work quoted are given in the main text, and reference should be made to the Bibliography on pages 168–9, where full details will be found.

ILLUSTRATIONS

ACKNOWLEDGMENTS

The two main sources on which I have drawn most heavily in this biographical study of Chabrier and his circle are, firstly, the invaluable collection of letters, edited and very fully annotated by the late Joseph Desaymard and published thirty-five years ago under the title *Chabrier d'après ses lettres*, and secondly the recent very reliable and authoritative *Life* of the composer by Madame Yvonne Tiénot, published in 1965. To this admirably documented and scholarly work I am greatly indebted, and I would like here to express to the author my gratitude for her help in clarifying various points, as well as for her very kind permission, and that of her publisher, Henri Lemoine et Cie, Paris, to reproduce some of the illustrations from her book which would not otherwise have been available. I am grateful, too, to Monsieur Marc Pincherle for allowing me to print some unpublished autograph letters in his possession and to the Société des Amis de l'Université de Clermont for permission to reproduce the photograph of Chabrier's birthplace first published in the *Revue d'Auvergne*. Finally I would like to thank Monsieur François Lesure and Madame Lebeau of the Music Department of the Bibliothèque Nationale for placing at my disposal the valuable collection of documents comprising the *Don Chabrier*, and for their help generally, and Mr Felix Aprahamian for allowing me to borrow from his library certain scores not readily obtainable elsewhere. My thanks are also due to the Courtauld Institute of Art, the Fogg Art Museum, Harvard University and Photographie Giraudon of Paris for permission to reproduce certain pictures from their collections.

INTRODUCTION

WHEN Emmanuel Chabrier was born in 1841 the century had so far produced only one French composer of real distinction in the person of Hector Berlioz, then aged thirty-eight and already famous as the composer of *Benvenuto Cellini, Roméo et Juliette* and the *Symphonie Fantastique*. Massenet and Fauré were not yet born; Saint-Saëns was a boy of six; while of the rising generation neither Gounod, Franck nor Lalo had as yet produced any major work. Nineteenth-century French music, in fact, was still in its infancy and was not destined to attain its full maturity for another fifty years or so, by which time the era of Debussy and Ravel had begun, and with it the birth of 'modern music'.

While Chabrier was growing up, the musical scene in Europe was dominated by the great figures of Brahms and Schumann, Liszt and Wagner; while it is interesting to note that his life-span of fifty-three years ran almost exactly parallel with that of Tchaikovsky, his senior by one year, who also died at the age of fifty-three.

Born during the reign of Louis-Philippe, Chabrier came to maturity under the Second Empire, and lived to see three Presidents of the Third Republic, MacMahon, Grévy and Carnot. Such was the political background of the period in which he lived and worked; but it is safe to say that politics was far from being a subject with which he was seriously concerned.

On the other hand, if we are to see Chabrier in his true perspective and understand the spirit of the age in which he lived and which is to some extent reflected in his music, it is desirable to know something about his social and artistic background and the formative influences which helped to shape his career.

He was a countryman by birth and descent, and came from a family whose ancestors had long been established in the Livradois region of Auvergne in Central France, in the *département* of Puy-de-Dôme. Here, in the little town of Ambert, where there had

been Chabriers for over a hundred years, Alexis Emmanuel was
born on 18th January 1841. His father, Jean, was a barrister; his
grandfather, Alexis, had been a magistrate, and his family tree
shows that the majority of his ancestors had been associated with
either the law, the Church or commerce. But there was one thing
all the Chabriers had in common, and that was a strong vein of
independence and fantasy, coupled with a lively intelligence and
a fair measure of that nervosity and ebullience for which the
natives of Auvergne have always been noted. For the important
thing to remember about Chabrier is that he was first and foremost
an 'Auvergnat'—a native of that highly individual province of
France which is unlike any other. Its inhabitants, in fact, are to
this day considered in France to be a race apart; hence the saying:
'Ni homme, ni femme, ni Auvergnat'—which could hardly be
more explicit. Chabrier, then, was a true son of the soil, and he must
be studied against this 'regional' background if we are to extract
from his personality and his work their full savour and significance.

   Although Auvergne has no special claim to be considered a
cultural centre or to have produced many famous artists, it is a
part of France in which the dance has always been cultivated with
enthusiasm and its traditional features jealously preserved—an
example being the famous 'Bourrée d'Auvergne' (immortalized
by Chabrier) which is a fairly elaborate dance-form of which both
the steps and music are firmly established and considered an
important part of the region's cultural life. But while this could
have been an environmental influence partly accounting for the
sudden emergence of a musical talent in a family in no way distinguished in the arts, it seems clear that, as always in such cases,
there must have been somewhere an hereditary influence also at
work, if not on the father's, then on the mother's side. And so
it is to Jean Chabrier's wife, *née* Marie-Anne-Evelina Durozay,
that we must turn now as being the most likely source of her son
Emmanuel's marked artistic tastes and temperament. She came
from Cusset, near Vichy in the Bourbonnais, bordering on the
Puy-de-Dôme, of a well-to-do family, and was brought up in a

milieu of some refinement where music and dancing were cultivated and enjoyed as part of a civilized life, while she herself appears to have been a woman of charm and distinction. There is little doubt then that it was from his mother that Emmanuel inherited the softer, more sensitive side of his nature; for, despite all his external ebullience and joviality, he was in reality, as we shall see, capable of great affection, kind and essentially good-hearted, devoted to his family and his friends, yet at the same time very highly strung. It was this side of his nature that Roland-Manuel (1951) had in mind when he discerned in Chabrier's music 'un extrême raffinement dans l'expression d'une immense tendresse'. In the more down-to-earth male members of his family, his father and uncles, for example, these traits were less conspicuous, but it was to them undoubtedly that Chabrier owed that spirit of sturdy independence and nonconformity that was one of his most appealing characteristics, and so forcefully reflected in his music. For the majority of his works bear the stamp of his highly original and engaging personality, full of high spirits and *joie de vivre* and intensely human. Truculent and boisterous he could be at times (and that, no doubt, is the popular image of the composer of the *Joyeuse Marche,* the 'bon diable en musique' as he has been called); but underneath lay a sensitive and dedicated artist who could say of himself: 'Never has an artist adored and sought to honour music more than I have; and no one has suffered more in doing so—and so shall I suffer to all eternity.'

In considering the case of Chabrier, who is too often dismissed as a minor composer of light music only, this aspect of his personality, and certain traits in his music which reveal it unmistakably, should be borne in mind; nor should it be forgotten that he was also a bold innovator who anticipated, in his harmonic language especially, many of the procedures which later became an integral part of the idiom of composers like Debussy and Ravel—both of whom, incidentally, thought very highly of him. Ravel indeed made no secret of his indebtedness to the composer of *Le Roi malgré lui* who, he claimed, had influenced him more than any other musician; while Debussy is reported to have said: 'Chabrier, Moussorgsky, Palestrina, voilà ce que j'aime' —at first sight a somewhat peculiar assortment, but it is easy to see what Debussy had in mind when uttering this *boutade*. Chabrier was also admired and cherished by many of his most distinguished contemporaries, including d'Indy, Chausson, Fauré and Duparc; and so far as one can see he had throughout his life no enemies. His interests, moreover, extended beyond music, and he counted many friends among the leading writers and poets and, especially, painters of his day, being an intimate friend of Manet and the possessor of an important collection of Impressionist paintings which he bought at a time when there were few who were capable of appreciating them at their just value. Chabrier, in short, was one of those interesting personalities we meet with from time to time in artistic, social or political history, the full significance of whose work is not always fully apparent until the extent to which it may have influenced others has been correctly assessed; and in this respect Chabrier shares with Erik Satie (another of his admirers) the distinction of having had a big influence on later musical developments in France. Most critics would be in agreement on this point; the late M. D. Calvocoressi, for example, who had an inside knowledge of French music, called Chabrier 'the direct forerunner of the modern school', while Francis Poulenc (1961) has stated that 'Chabrier represents, with Fauré, Debussy, Ravel and Satie, what is best in French music since 1880'. And the wise and perspicacious Charles Koechlin, the *éminence grise* at whose feet have sat so many of France's leading composers, did not hesitate to declare (1930) that 'Chabrier n'est pas seulement un grand musicien—l'un de nos plus grands musiciens—il reste un incompris, et de bien des gens'.

This book, then, is an attempt to place Chabrier in his true perspective, to find out why he has so long been 'incompris', and to portray the man and the musician in the light of his achievements and in relation to the music of our time.

CHAPTER ONE

Early years in Auvergne—Studies law in Paris—Enters Ministry of Interior—Studies music in spare time—First contacts with Parisian artistic and literary world—Friendship and collaboration with Verlaine—Joins the Petit Bayreuth *group of ardent Wagnerites.*

HE RECEIVED his early schooling locally, and had his first piano lessons at the age of six. In the light of what we know about Chabrier's subsequent career and the lifelong interest taken by the composer of *España* in Spain and everything Spanish, it seems both appropriate and significant that he should have received his first lessons in music from two Spanish musicians who had settled in his native town. The reason for their presence there was as follows. In 1830 King Ferdinand VII of Spain, by abolishing the Salic Law, had secured the throne for his daughter Isabelle, thereby excluding from the succession his brother Don Carlos. This led to the Carlist rising of 1834, ending in the defeat in 1839 of the Pretender's supporters, many of whom then crossed the Pyrenees and settled in France, for the most part in the central provinces and Auvergne. These *émigrés* included two Spanish musicians one of whom, Antonio Pitarch y Fabra, had been the bandmaster of his regiment. He settled in Le Puy-en-Velay, where he became organist of the cathedral and conductor of the local orchestra and choral societies, as well as being responsible for all the music taught in schools throughout the district. He was eventually joined by his friend and fellow countryman Manuel Zaporta, who found employment as a piano teacher in the little town of Ambert, where he soon made a name for himself, as he was not only a first-class musician but also, it seems, a man of great charm and distinction.

And so it was not long before the Chabrier parents had entrusted him with their little son Emmanuel, who already showed signs of possessing considerable pianistic talent. It seems that the

boy also had lessons from Antonio Pitarch's brother Mateo, who
came to take Manuel Zaporta's place when the latter, having
amassed enough money for the voyage, decided to widen his
horizon and emigrate to South America where he eventually had
a successful career as a pianist. Zaporta made a rich marriage,
and returned with his wife to Europe, settling in Paris where he
died in 1902 at the age of eighty. Mateo Pitarch ended his days
at Ambert, but one of his daughters became a celebrated singer,
appearing with success at La Scala in Milan.

This early contact with Spain in the persons of his two Spanish
music masters must have made a lasting impression on the young
Chabrier, but he was not with them for very long, as when he was
eleven years old his parents moved to Clermont-Ferrand so that
he could attend the Lycée Blaise Pascal in that town. Here he
remained for another five years until the family moved to Paris,
and during that time he continued his musical studies, notably
with a Polish musician named Tarnowski, and perpetrated his
first childish compositions, none of which, according to those
who have seen them, including Alfred Cortot, showed the slightest
signs of any real talent or originality. They consisted mostly of
quadrilles, waltzes, polkas and suchlike with picturesque
titles such as La Chute des feuilles, L'Echo du verger, Les Bords de l'Alma,
full of clichés and so devoid of any real invention that, as Cortot
remarks (1948), 'it is difficult to imagine, when perusing these
puerile pages, that they marked the apparition of one of the most
highly personal and profoundly original musical temperaments
of our time'.

Although quite willing for his son to continue his musical
studies as a sideline, Chabrier père, himself a lawyer, was determined that Emmanuel should follow in his footsteps and study
law with a view to making his career as a civil servant. Accord-
ingly, when the boy was sixteen the family moved to Paris where,
after studying for four years at the Lycée St Louis, Emmanuel,
having passed his bachot and obtained his law degree, entered the
Ministry of the Interior (the French Home Office) as a junior

clerk. There for the next eighteen years he was to remain, but from now on he was to devote all his spare time to music. He took piano lessons from Edouard Wolff, a distinguished Polish pianist who had been closely associated with Chopin, and studied composition with Aristide Hignard, a composer today forgotten but well thought of at the time and the author of a *Hamlet* which was considered by many to be superior to Ambroise Thomas's opera—though that in itself perhaps would hardly constitute a certificate of the highest merit. For was it not this composer that Chabrier made fun of later in his famous witticism: 'Il y a trois espèces de musique: la bonne, la mauvaise, et celle d'Ambroise Thomas . . .'? But although Chabrier no doubt had a more extensive musical training than most amateurs, yet in the last resort he was largely self-taught, spending many hours in studying the scores of the great masters and often copying them out in full, as he did, for example, with the Overture to *Tannhäuser*, marking his copy in blue pencil with these words: 'Musique de *Tannhäuser* copiée par moi pour apprendre l'orchestre.' In this way he managed to teach himself a lot about orchestration and the techniques of composition which helped him to develop his own very personal style—although he confided to a friend in later life, when he was already forty-five, that composing was never easy for him: 'Tout me coûte beaucoup de travail; je n'ai pas ce qu'on appelle de la facilité.'

And so it is true that in some respects Chabrier remained (as those jealous of him were never tired of pointing out) an amateur all his life and was handicapped, having taken up music as a profession so late, by having never acquired completely what Cortot (1948) called 'that independence and facility for writing music which even the humblest of note-spinners can learn if they have benefited from the discipline imposed by scholastic studies at an early age'. Yet it is precisely this freedom from any hint of scholasticism that gives Chabrier's music its peculiar freshness and spontaneity, a unique mixture of artfulness and artlessness; and it is a remarkable tribute to his skill and resourcefulness that, in spite of the fact that writing music did not come easily to him, this is never allowed to show in the finished product; whatever happens, his music always flows. He was over thirty before he had published anything of importance, and nearly forty before he gave up his regular occupation in the Ministry to devote himself entirely to music; and as he was only fifty-three when he died his output was necessarily restricted in quantity.

From the brief outline of Chabrier's childhood and early student years it can be seen, then, that the first twenty years or so of his life were, on the whole, singularly uneventful, and apparently so free from the stresses and strains with which a budding genius so often has to contend that it is all the more surprising that in fact they turned out to be the prelude to a career of exceptional brilliance and achievement. A short one, it it true, but long enough to have ensured for Chabrier a very special place in musical history.

Had his parents not decided to move to Paris when he was a boy, it is questionable whether the young Chabrier would ever have found the stimulus he needed to make him take up music as a career; nor is it likely that he would have made the valuable contacts in the literary and artistic world which not only widened very considerably his intellectual horizon but provided him with new interests and many lasting and valued friendships. It is clear, however, that Chabrier lost no time after his entry into the Ministry in making new acquaintances; and although he was as yet unknown as a composer (though possibly his reputation as a pianist and former child prodigy had preceded him) it was not long before he had somehow found his way into the *salons* frequented by many of the poets, painters and musicians who were then prominent in Parisian society. It seems unlikely that his father, who had by then obtained a post as legal adviser to one of the railway administrations, could have been much use to him in that direction; it was more probably through his mother—who, as we have seen, was artistically inclined—that he obtained

his first introductions into a world in which he was soon to
become very much at home and destined to play a prominent
part. For, in addition to his lively disposition and sociable
instincts, the young Emmanuel was blessed with a keen intelligence, and was interested in all forms of artistic experience and
activities. Indeed at one time he had seriously thought of taking
up painting as a profession; and it was this instinctive feeling
for the plastic arts that made him something of a connoisseur
where painting was concerned, and led him not only to frequent
the society of painters but also to buy up their pictures whenever
he could for the pleasure of possessing them and in order to
encourage those artists whose work he felt instinctively would
have lasting value. In this way he amassed a collection of pictures
by the leading Impressionist painters of the day at a time when
they were far from being fashionable but looked upon almost as
anti-art and offending against all the canons of what the 'Establishment' of the day considered to be good taste. For instance,
at a sale of their pictures at the Hôtel Drouot organized in 1875
by Monet, Berthe Morisot, Sisley and Renoir the police had to
intervene to disperse a crowd of Beaux Arts students manifesting
against this *avant-garde* painting which so shocked the pundits
that a critic in *Le Figaro* actually described the exhibition as a
'disaster' and referred to the artists as 'a band of five or six
lunatics including a woman, who get hold of a canvas, some paint
and some brushes, splash on a few colours haphazard and sign
the result'.

Four years later, on the occasion of the fourth Impressionist
exhibition, Chabrier bought several Monets, and in the meantime
had made the acquaintance of Renoir, and also of Manet with
whom he struck up a lifelong friendship. After the latter's death
in 1884 (he died in Chabrier's arms) Chabrier, with the aid of a
legacy which his wife had received, bought from the artist's
studio a number of important canvases, including the famous
Un Bar aux Folies-Bergère, which he acquired for 5,850 francs. He
also sat to Manet for his portrait on two occasions, one being

an oil painting executed in 1881, and the other a pastel dating
from the previous year. Manet had already painted him as one of
the top-hatted figures in his well-known picture *Bal masqué à
l'Opéra* in 1873. He was also portrayed by Fantin-Latour as the
central figure in the group of musicians in *Autour du piano*
(exhibited in the Paris Salon in 1885), and was presented by the
artist with lithographs of this picture and of Fantin's other
celebrated group (this time of poets) entitled *Un Atelier aux Batignolles*.

Other portraits of Chabrier by artists who were his friends
include a crayon drawing by Tissot inscribed 'A mon ami
Chabrier, James Tissot, 9 Obre. 1861', and one by Marcellin
Desboutin, a great friend of Manet's who, incidentally, was
Degas's model for the male figure in his picture *L'Absinthe*. Degas
also painted Chabrier, who can be seen in a box at the Opera in
the picture *L'Orchestre* in which the central figure was the artist's
friend, the bassoonist Désiré Dihau. There is also a well-known
bust of him by the sculptor Constantin Meunier, and finally the
famous portrait-caricature by Edouard Detaille in which Chabrier,
clad in a voluminous mustard-coloured ulster, with flowing
scarf and wearing a top-hat, is seated at the piano in an evidently
expansive mood. This could be taken as an illustration of his
fellow composer and friend Alfred Bruneau's description (1900)
of Chabrier at the piano:

> He played the piano as no one has ever played it before, or
> ever will. The sight of Chabrier, in a drawing-room full of
> elegant women, advancing towards the fragile instrument and
> then playing his *España* in a blaze of broken strings, hammers
> reduced to pulp and splintered keys, was indescribably droll,
> and a spectacle of truly epic grandeur.

If then, as we have seen, Chabrier was unusually well served
by his friends the painters, he on the other hand returned the
compliment handsomely and amassed during his short life a
remarkably fine collection of contemporary pictures—an achieve-

ment which surely puts him in a class apart among musicians whose interest in the visual arts rarely extends to buying pictures on a large scale and, what is more, in defiance of fashionable trends. It is some indication of Chabrier's unerring flair and natural good taste that when his own collection was sold after his death in 1894 it included no less than eleven Manets, eight Monets, six Renoirs, two Sisleys, one Cézanne, two Forains and, strangely enough, an unfinished picture of a Spanish dancer by Sargent. (A complete list, with further details, of the pictures in Chabrier's collection will be found in Chapter Ten.) M. Roger Delage (1963*d*) gives a very full and interesting account of Chabrier's relations with contemporary painters.

While Chabrier was thus enjoying the society and friendship of the leading *avant-garde* painters of the day he was also losing no time in making the acquaintance of their opposite numbers in the world of music and literature, being again attracted instinctively to all the writers and musicians who had the reputation of being 'advanced'—innovators like d'Indy and Fauré, Chausson and Duparc (for that is what they were in the eighteen-sixties and -seventies) and, in the world of letters, Verlaine, Mallarmé, Zola, Alphonse Daudet, Jean Moréas, Jean Richepin and Villiers de l'Isle-Adam. The latter, who was something of a musician as well as a poet, and had even tried his hand at composition, took a few lessons from Chabrier which he acknowledged gracefully in a copy of his *Contes cruels* dedicated 'A mon ami Emmanuel Chabrier, son apprenti musicien de bonne volonté et son cordial admirateur'.

But it was above all with Verlaine that Chabrier was most closely associated. It is probable that they first met either in the *salon* of the Marquise de Ricard which was then the headquarters of the so-called 'Parnassian' poets, of whom her son Xavier de Ricard and Catulle Mendès were the recognized leaders, or else at the house of the celebrated Bohemian hostess Nina de Callias, which was a great meeting-place for any members of Parisian society who were interested in the arts.[1] The two men were

almost the same age, and evidently felt a mutual attraction. At
all events Chabrier soon began going regularly to the Verlaines'
house, for we find him noting in his copy of the poet's *Jadis et
naguère*: 'Pendant deux ou trois ans, de 1860 à 1863, rue Lécluze,
aux Batignolles, j'allai dîner chez Madame Verlaine presque tous
les samedis.' Moreover this friendship soon resulted in a collaboration between the musician and the poet which took the form
of two little *opéra-bouffes*, evidently of a very light nature, entitled
Fisch-ton-Kan and *Vaucochard et fils Ier*, which were, in fact, never
published and probably only privately performed, if at all, in
their authors' lifetime.[2] Francis Poulenc, however, records in
his monograph on Chabrier that some fragments (all that remains)
from these early works were publicly performed at the Salle de
l'Ancien Conservatoire in Paris on 22nd April 1941 (thanks to
the co-operation of Chabrier's daughter-in-law, Mme Bretton-
Chabrier), and that he himself played the piano in *Fisch-ton-Kan*,
while the late Roger Desormière, a great admirer of Chabrier,
conducted *Vaucochard*.[3]

These two little works, the fruit of a collaboration between
Chabrier and Verlaine, must be considered then, in a sense, as
Chabrier's *début* as a composer, though as they date from 1863
and 1864 they could give only the faintest indication of the lines
on which Chabrier was likely to develop. Poulenc mentions an air
from one of them, *Chanson de l'homme armé*, as being 'authentic
Chabrier', and from the point of view of prosody, a '*trouvaille*';
but his career as a composer cannot be said to have started
effectively until ten years later with the publication in 1873 of
an *Impromptu* in C major for piano, dedicated to Mme Edouard
Manet, which Cortot describes as 'a work full of invention,
rhythmic ingenuity and harmonic subtleties', which indeed it is,
with every bar bearing the unmistakable imprint of Chabrier's
spontaneous unconventionality. But these early *opéra-bouffes* are
worthy of mention, if only because they prompted the well-
known poem of Verlaine (in the collection *Amour* of 1888)
beginning:

Chabrier, nous faisions, un ami cher et moi,
Des paroles pour vous qui leur donniez des ailes,
Et tous trois frémissions quand, pour bénir nos zèles
Passait l'*Ecce Deus* et le je ne sais quoi.

Chez ma mère charmante et divinement bonne
Votre génie improvisait au piano,
Et c'était tout autour comme un brûlant anneau
De sympathie et d'aise qui rayonne.

(Chabrier, a dear friend[4] and I wrote for you words to which
you gave wings, and we all three trembled when there came to
bless our efforts the *Ecce Deus* and things which cannot be
expressed. As in the presence of my charming and saintly
mother your genius was improvising at the piano, it was as if a
glowing ring of sympathy and bliss was radiating all round us.)

and ending with the line:

'Le souvenir des frais instants de paix profonde.'
('The memory of those fresh moments of perfect peace.')

But all this time it must be remembered that Chabrier still
had no intention of taking up music as a career although, as we
have seen, he practised the piano assiduously and spent many
hours copying scores of composers whom he admired. The idea
of giving up his position in the Ministry had not yet occurred to
him; indeed it is on record that he confided to a friend that in
his opinion music was not a profession, and 'would not bring in
enough to pay for one's drinking water. Whereas at the Ministry,
thanks to the protection of a high-up cousin of mine, I shall soon
be earning 100 francs a month. And at sixty one gets a pension'.
It seems paradoxical that a musician who was to make a name for
himself above all as an anti-orthodox, anti-conventional, anti-
academic individualist could ever have had such a prosaic,
unadventurous outlook as a young man, or have waited, with all
his innate talent, until he was over thirty before deciding to

devote his life to what he was evidently put into the world to do—make music. Rimsky-Korsakov and Roussel, among others, were both well over twenty before taking up music as a career, but of all the late starters Chabrier must hold the record. (In this context one thinks inevitably of Chabrier's famous repartee when a rather insipid fellow composer, Benjamin Godard, remarked to him one day: 'What a pity, my dear Emmanuel, that you took up music so late,' only to be countered with the instant retort: 'And what a pity, my dear Benjamin, that you started so early. . . .')

Nevertheless, during his first ten years at the Ministry, Chabrier did not waste his spare time and found no difficulty in entering the charmed circle of artists, writers and musicians who were enlivening Paris at that time and who seem to have accepted him from the first as one of their own kind. Among those with whom he became friendly were eccentrics like the Bohemian Cabaner, and the enigmatic Charles de Sivry, Verlaine's brother-in-law, with whom he used to play piano duets. This de Sivry was the son, by a previous marriage, of Mme Antoinette Mauté, Verlaine's mother-in-law, and half-brother of Mathilde Mauté, Verlaine's unfortunate young wife, and in a rather curious way was instrumental in helping Debussy, when still a young boy, to get the proper musical education he needed at a time when his family was in serious difficulties. It was during the insurrection of the Commune, after the Franco-Prussian war, in which both he and Verlaine were involved, that de Sivry met Debussy's father Manuel, who was then Captain de Bussy, a company commander in the revolutionary army. After their defeat Manuel was arrested and imprisoned; but, knowing de Sivry's musical background and his connection with the Mauté-Verlaine families, he succeeded in enlisting his interest in his son Claude's exceptional musical gifts, with the result that Mme Mauté was soon giving the boy piano lessons (she was an excellent musician herself and is said to have known Chopin) and arranging for him to enter the Paris Conservatoire.

Charles de Sivry often played the piano at the famous cabaret the *Chat Noir*, and it is probable that Chabrier sometimes accompanied his friend Verlaine on his visits there, as the cabaret was much frequented by artists and writers at that time. He would have met Cabaner, that bizarre and eccentric poet, at another cabaret, *La Nouvelle Athènes*, and would surely have appreciated the wit and bizarre humour of the man who once said that it would take three military bands to give the impression of silence in music. . . .

In this way, and in this kind of society, Chabrier spent the first ten or fifteen years of what we might call his period of gestation and initiation into the artistic world of Paris. Gestation, because all the time he was studying and learning and allowing to ripen slowly within him the seeds of his own very personal creative genius which was not yet ready to flower; and initiation, because he was almost daily in contact with some of the best minds and talents in the world of music, literature and the plastic arts.

Moreover, in addition to the Impressionists, the Symbolists and the Parnassians there was yet another 'movement', and a very powerful one, to be reckoned with which was to have a decisive influence, more decisive indeed than any of the others, on Chabrier's future career—and that was the modish craze for Wagner, rife in all Parisian *avant-garde* circles, literary as well as musical, to which he inevitably succumbed and which proved eventually, as we shall see, to be the catalysing influence which made him decide to give up everything and devote his life to music. He did not actually resign from the Ministry until 1879, when he was thirty-eight, as a direct result of hearing *Tristan* for the first time; but he had been involved some time before that in the inner circle of fervent Wagnerites known as the *Petit Bayreuth*, and sometimes conducted arrangements for small orchestra of the master's works at meetings which took place at the house of the *Petit Bayreuth*'s founder, the Parisian magistrate Antoine Lascoux. The seed was sown; it was only a matter of time before it would come to fruition.

CHAPTER TWO

Visits Holland and Belgium—Plans for opera Jean Hunyade *unrealized —Franco-Prussian war and marriage—Production of* L'Etoile *turning point in his career—Success of* Une Education manquée.

THE FINANCIAL situation of the Chabriers was probably that of an average French bourgeois family under the Second Empire living on an income ranging, it has been estimated, from six to fifteen thousand francs a year, which could be either wholly un-earned or supplemented by emoluments from one of the liberal professions. In the Chabriers' case, though the family, as we have seen, had private means, both father and son, after the move to Paris, were in paid employment, so that it may be assumed that they were more or less comfortably off. It was therefore possible for Emmanuel, though only a humble employee at the Ministry, to indulge from time to time in his great passion—foreign travel, which in those days was a luxury inaccessible, unlike today, to the majority of middle-class Frenchmen who usually had to content themselves with a summer holiday at the seaside or at some spa or mountain resort. Chabrier's desire to travel was only another symptom of his innate and insatiable curiosity about everything life had to offer and his interest in people and things which he looked at always with an artist's eye. He was an excellent letter writer and wielded a fluent pen, so it is fortunate that a great many of his letters have been preserved, for it is through them that his personality is projected in a way that seems to supplement ideally the impression that is made upon us by his music.[1] One of his first trips abroad was to Holland and Belgium when he was a young man of twenty-four, and the letters he wrote to his parents on this occasion show with what a keen eye he observed the scene around him and how vividly and unaffectedly he recorded his impressions and his uninhibited delight in all that he saw and heard. The following letter, written from Rotter-

dam (the year was 1865) is a good example of his epistolary style
and of his lively temperament:

. . . Thanks be to God, I haven't been bored for a second so
far!—The Hague was most enjoyable, but how I wished my
poor J., who's mad about painting, could have been with me!
A museum no bigger than a handkerchief, but what treasures
it contains! Paul Potter's *Oxen*, Rembrandt's *The Anatomy
Lesson*, several Van der Elsts, Ruysdaels, Van Ostades and
Hobbemas, and two delicious Van Dycks. Here in Rotterdam
the museum was burned down a few years ago. It seems it
contained a quantity of masterpieces of the Dutch school—
what an irreparable loss!

At Scheveningen, where I went twice, the ladies are more
modest than last year. A nudity from time to time, the glimpse
of a torso here and there, but the sea is always rough and inter-
rupts your admiration; *pouf!* here comes a wave, and there's
nothing to be seen. Also, it's bitterly cold.

In the evening, in the Park, I heard an excellent military
band—all the same, Paris is hard to beat! Last night I went to
the Opera in Rotterdam where they were giving, in German,
Die Hugenotten von Meijerbeer—note the vintage spelling;
not bad, but they tended to skip the difficult passages, especially in the choruses. The quarrel scene was ruined, and in the
fifth act, when Raoul, Marcel and Valentine are going to be
shot, the arquebuses failed to go off, and this made the audience
laugh. As for the ballets! . . . I wonder how they'd compare
with Nantes or Bordeaux, for example, because Rotterdam,
make no mistake, has a population of some 130,000—quite
a deep hole, in fact. . . . Today is Sunday, and I'm going to
the Park to hear *la grosse musick*; after that a frugal meal, and
to end with no doubt some wretched *café chantant* since there's
opera only twice a week. Mamma, your suggestion is a very
sound one, but unfortunately I can't do as you say; if I drink
wine with my dinner my dinner will cost me five francs; if I

take beer it's only a florin!! In three weeks I don't think
there'll be time for me to fall a victim to obesity!

Tomorrow I'm off to Antwerp. I hope the Gossi family
will do their stuff—between ourselves, I sincerely hope so for
I haven't laid hands on a piano for six days. My fingers itch
painfully, and I find myself sometimes drumming on my hat,
on the table, on the back of my neighbour or on anything
handy. In Amsterdam, let me tell you, I followed a bunch of
commercial travellers into a disreputable café where there
wasn't a soul—except a piano! I made a dash for it, and for the
next quarter of an hour I entertained five or six types who
listened open-mouthed, but of course I had to play for them,
so as not to be taken for an imbecile, the *Carnaval de Venise,*
the *Chalet* and *O mon Fernand* and other such drivel; but at
least I was playing, that was the main thing. Then people
began to come in, and I left the instrument. Anyway, I didn't
really disgrace myself! There are some fortunate people who
are always having adventures. I'm looking for adventures all
day long and for part of the night, but never find anything—
I'm lucky if I can find my way. Finally I end up one evening
at Scheveningen in what I suppose is the Hôtel des Bains,
and there's a great brute of a piano standing there with its
arms folded while a few not too bad-looking ladies are sitting
reading or doing embroidery or playing whist. I enter; invite
the ladies to dance; we have a very gay evening; I get up a
collection for the poor local fishermen, and am altogether a
great success. There's nothing extraordinary about all this.
We'd have done just the same if J. had been there; he'd have
danced like a teetotum or else turned over the pages for me,
as he pleased. When there are two of you one has much more
self-confidence. But all alone . . . ! Never mind, I'm quite
content. . . . Mamma, it's nice of you to wait for my return
before you go away; now you'll have time to embrace your
old

                                                    Emmanuel.

In another letter to his parents, written this time from Brussels, Chabrier speaks of going to see *Freischütz* and of driving round the city in a *fiacre* 'so as to get an idea of the general layout'; but to allay any suspicions his parents might have that he was over-spending, he is careful to impress upon them that the cost of living in the Belgian capital was very low: 'My room, including service, 2 frs., breakfast with coffee and bread and butter 0.75, and dinner 2 frs. including a half bottle of good wine. And with that, I can afford as many theatres, beers and even *fiacres* as I like. . . .'

Shortly after this trip abroad Chabrier, perhaps stimulated by what he had seen and heard, conceived the idea of writing an opera on the subject of Hunyadi Janos—an ambitious project indeed, considering that up to now he had produced no serious works and was quite without experience of the theatre. For the libretto he turned to one Henri Fouquier, a writer who had been connected with the theatre but had now turned politician, who eventually supplied him with two acts to work on, although clearly some time elapsed before he consented to do so. For we find Chabrier writing to him somewhat apprehensively, but at the same time with a certain insistence, asking for a definite yes or no with regard to their collaboration:

It's me again, my dear friend—I'd like to say collaborator; I called on you, but the concierge told me you had just gone off to the country, and I didn't like to ask her where you'd gone as I've no intention of pursuing you everywhere just to talk about a certain Hunyadi. And yet we must get this cleared up; I bet I'm boring you already with my Hungarian. If so, I'm sure you'd be frank enough not to hide from me the awful truth—out with it then, I'll be brave—but if only you knew how paralysed I am for want of a libretto. To sum up, then: (*a*) Are we going to work together? (*b*) Don't let's get on each other's nerves but decide once for all what we want to do.

Yours,

Emmanuel.

In the end he got his libretto, but either because it did not inspire him or because he was dissatisfied with his own efforts, Chabrier soon gave it up, leaving only some sketches which, however, in the opinion of Francis Poulenc, who had studied the MS., showed promise and contained certain striking details of scoring which definitely foreshadowed the Chabrier to come. In any case the composer himself did not altogether disown this early effort, for he bequeathed the MS. to his son Marcel, and added a note stating that the music contained two themes which he had used in his operas *Gwendoline* and *Briséïs*, underlining them in the score.[2]

Two years after this abortive operatic venture Chabrier lost both his parents, their deaths being separated by only a few weeks. He was now twenty-eight and had still produced nothing of any consequence; eight years were to elapse before he had his first real success, with his operetta *L'Etoile*. And if these eight years had been entirely uneventful it would have been legitimate to skip them. But the biography of an artist is also the biography of a man, and it is therefore the duty of a biographer to record events which were important to the artist as a man, though not necessarily reflected in his art. And among such events marriage is one that should surely be included, while on another plane the effect on a man—and especially an artist—of his country being involved in a disastrous war is also something that deserves at least a passing mention. In Chabrier's case the war was of course the Franco-Prussian, which broke out the year following the deaths of his father and mother; three years later he married Alice Dejean, by whom he had two sons, Marcel born in 1874 and André born in 1878. (A third son died in infancy.) His marriage was a happy one, marred only by his wife's poor health which forced her to lead a very inactive life. The war for Chabrier meant not military service, since he was a Government employee, but exile from Paris, obliged as he was to follow the Government first to Tours, then to Bordeaux and finally Versailles. He was not entirely alone, because his faithful old nurse—his Nanine as he called her—stayed on to keep house for him, and there was a touching relationship between them which is reflected in the many letters he wrote to her on various occasions, treating her always as a dearly loved member of his family. During his absence from Paris in the war years Nanine was left in charge of his home, and his concern for her is shown in the following brief note he wrote to her from Versailles during the terrible period of the Commune:

My dear,

I am at Versailles. I beg you to keep an eye on everything; don't lose your head, and go on loving me as I love you. Look after your own safety first; nothing else matters.

Your

Emmanuel.

No harm came to either of them as it happened, and once the war was over Chabrier settled down again in Paris and as before continued to work at music in his spare time. That he was still interested in writing for the theatre is shown by the fact that in 1872 he was one of three composers who wrote the music for an operetta in three acts called *Le Service obligatoire* which was performed at a private club, the *Cercle des Mirlitons*, in the Place Vendôme on 27th December and reported in *Le Gaulois* in its issue of 30th December. The identity of the three composers, whose initials only—J.C., E.C. and R.B.—appeared on the programme, was revealed in this newspaper: they were Jules Coste (an amateur), Emmanuel Chabrier and René de Boisdeffre (1838–1906), a minor composer of some distinction and the author of various chamber works as well as a symphony and a cantata on *The Song of Songs*. Unfortunately no trace of the music for this operetta remains, and indeed its very existence was unknown until unearthed by one of Chabrier's biographers, Georges Servières, who published his findings in *La Revue Musicale* of July 1921. Though probably unimportant from a purely

musical point of view, the fact that Chabrier, still unknown to the
general public, was invited to collaborate in a production of this
kind, which evidently had some social undertones, showed that
he already had his admirers in certain strata of Parisian society.
However, his first real opportunity for a breakthrough was not
to come until five years later as the result of a chance meeting,
in the studio of a painter friend, with two famous librettists who
had already made a name for themselves through their collaboration with Charles Lecocq in two of his operettas, *Giroflé-Girofla*
(1874) and *La Petite mariée* (1875). They were Leterrier and
Vanloo; and at that time they were on the look-out for a young
composer to write the music for their latest piece, a light, almost
farcical comedy entitled *L'Etoile*. They had heard some songs and
piano pieces by Chabrier which convinced them that here was the
man they were seeking. He accepted their offer on the spot,
started work almost immediately, and in a few months' time his
score was ready. And so, on 28th November 1877, *L'Etoile* had
its first performance at the Théâtre des Bouffes-Parisiens, and
Chabrier became famous overnight. For the piece was an instant
success with both the public and the critics, and Chabrier at last
had proved that he was something more than a gifted amateur.
Yet, in spite of every ingredient that seemed to guarantee for it
a long and successful run, the piece was taken off after only
forty-eight performances; the ill luck that, as we shall see,
ruined every one of Chabrier's operatic ventures had already set
in and, as in every other case, had nothing to do with the merits
or demerits of the work itself, but was due to entirely extraneous
circumstances. On this occasion the reason given for ending the
run of *L'Etoile* was the illness of a leading member of the cast;
but it has been suggested that the real reason may have been that
by the terms of their contract the authors and composer would
have stood to gain more than the director of the theatre after
the fiftieth performance. In any case, whatever the reason for the
shortness of its initial run may have been, the surprising thing is
that *L'Etoile* has had so few performances since that date. It was,

however, produced at the Opéra-Comique during the Occupation in 1941 under the direction of the late Roger Désormière. But the initiative of the then Director of the Paris Opéras, Jacques Rouché, seems to have been ill timed for, as Poulenc (1961) remarks sadly: 'Malheureusement l'époque n'était pas au rire!'

Nevertheless, it is strange that a work of such irresistible charm and profound musicality, the model of everything a light opera should be, has been so undeservedly neglected. No doubt its singularly idiotic and 'dated' libretto has been a serious handicap, but the score abounds in the most delightful music, while from the point of view of orchestration and harmony it is infinitely superior to the majority of operettas of the period (though in fairness, perhaps, an exception should be made for those of Offenbach and Lecocq, whose workmanship is polished but less adventurous than that of Chabrier).

There is no distinguishable 'plot'; only a succession of scenes and set pieces in which characters rejoicing in such names as Ouf I (the King), Laoula and Lazuli (the 'hero' and 'heroine'), Hérisson de Porc Epic (Hedgehog), Sirocco, Tapioca (courtiers), and Oasis, Youka, Asphodèle, Zinnia and Koukoula (chorus ladies) perform various antics and sing a number of charming airs and couplets. Among the most delightful of these may be cited the fragrant little *Romance de l'Etoile*, beautifully written with a simple elegance that lifts it above the ordinary level of 'light music'; the gracefully turned *Couplets de la rose*; the amusing and lively *Rondeau du colporteur*: 'Oui, je suis Lazuli, le colporteur joli, le fournisseur des dames . . .'; and the irresistibly comical *Duo de la Chartreuse verte*, a parody of an Italian operatic aria à la Donizetti which, incidentally, was one of the numbers which especially delighted Debussy. Debussy, indeed, was one of Chabrier's most ardent admirers, and we are told that 'one of his delights was to sing to his own accompaniment sometimes the whole of *L'Etoile* from beginning to end, being wildly enthusiastic over its "trouvailles fantaisistes" and "truculent entrain"'. (René Peter, 1944.)

Romance de l'Etoile

All this is light music at its best; completely unvulgar, unfailingly musical and delightfully spontaneous and uninhibited. After taking a close look at this unjustly neglected little work one can well understand what moved the late Charles Koechlin (1946) to declare, in making an eloquent plea for music that need not

necessarily be 'profound' (citing *en passant* Saint-Saëns's remark
in defence of Massenet: 'Il n'est pas profond? Et après?') that
certain works of Gounod and Chabrier—*Une Education manquée,
L'Etoile, Philémon et Baucis, Le Médecin malgré lui*—are, 'by their
charming musicality, the justness of their accent, their supreme
(and so French) intelligence, their marvellous orchestration—in
a word, by their Quality—nothing less than masterpieces'. Very
similar views have been expressed by Stravinsky (1947):

> It is curious to note that it is a musician who proclaimed him-
> self a Wagnerite, the Frenchman Chabrier, who was able in
> these difficult times to maintain the sound tradition of dramatic
> art, and who excelled in the *genre* of French *opéra-comique* when
> Wagnerism was all the rage, along with a few of his com-
> patriots. Is it not this tradition that survives in the bouquet
> of masterpieces called *Le Médecin malgré lui, La Colombe,
> Philémon et Baucis* of Gounod; *Lakmé, Coppélia, Sylvia* of
> Delibes; *Carmen; Le Roi malgré lui, L'Etoile* of Chabrier . . . ?

Two years after the short-lived triumph of *L'Etoile* Chabrier,
again on a libretto by Leterrier and Vanloo, wrote the music for
a one-act farcical sketch, or *saynète, Une Education manquée*, which
was produced at the *Cercle de la Presse* in Paris in May 1879. (As
recently as 1934 it was revived by Diaghilev in a version with
recitatives composed by Darius Milhaud and scenery and costumes
designed by Juan Gris.) The subject of this somewhat frivolous
little sketch is as follows: The young Gontran de Boismassif has
a learned tutor, one Pausanias, who has taught him everything a
young man needs to know in science and the arts—mythology,
metallurgy, agronomy, heliography, etc.—but has failed to explain
to his pupil, as Gontran discovers to his great chagrin on his
wedding night, the precise nature of the duties which his bride
might not unreasonably expect him to perform on that occasion.
Furious, he sends for Pausanias and orders him to find a remedy for
this deplorable state of affairs without delay. Fortunately, however, no sooner has Pausanias turned his back than a violent

thunderstorm breaks out which drives his terrified bride into
Gontran's arms, thus ensuring that before very long he will have
found the solution to his problem. . . .

What we have to admire here is the way in which Chabrier's
music transcends the triviality of this libretto (which Poulenc
calls 'a perfect example of the purest Louis Quinze chocolate-
box style') transforming it into a work of art in which (to quote
Poulenc again) 'there is not a single page which does not bear the
imprint of a master's hand'.

From now on Chabrier may be said to have 'arrived'; his long
period of apprenticeship and study was now behind him, and he
began to be recognized for what he was—a composer of quite
remarkable originality, and a new star to be added to the galaxy
of French nineteenth-century musicians who, to do them justice,
were now beginning to revise their early opinion of Chabrier as
being merely a gifted amateur. That there may have been a touch
of the amateur in him throughout his career is not, however,
something that ought to be held against him; for are not all the
greatest artists in some degree, and in the best sense, amateurs?
This was a truth that Erik Satie was never tired of proclaiming
(thus underlining the essential quality that distinguishes the true
creative spirit from the mere technician) and a theme on which
he expatiated to some length in a paper he published in *Les
Feuilles Libres* in 1922, defending Albert Roussel (his old teacher
at the *Schola Cantorum*) against the charge of being 'only an amateur'
brought against him by a former 'Prix de Rome'. Satie quite
properly inveighs against the absurd prestige attaching to this
prize, and concludes sarcastically that

> since neither César Franck, d'Indy, Lalo, Chabrier nor
> Chausson were 'Prix de Rome', they must therefore be con-
> sidered 'amateurs'. . . . Why must music alone of the arts be
> saddled with so much academic officialdom when both paint-
> ing and literature can dispense with it? . . . With a united
> voice I cry: Long live the Amateurs!

A view with which it would be difficult to find fault when one bears in mind the debt music owes to 'amateurs' of the calibre of Mussorgsky, Borodin, Gesualdo, Satie or Charles Ives, none of whom can be accused of being 'amateurish' in the pejorative sense of the term, implying sloppy workmanship and technical inefficiency. Autodidacts may be amateurs in the sense that they lack professional training, but this does not in itself preclude them from being artists who may well have more to contribute than many of their better schooled but less imaginative *confrères*. There are times when vision is more important than virtuosity.

In more ways than one the year of his success with *Une Education manquée* was an important landmark in Chabrier's career, for it was in this year that he at last took the decision he had put off for so long, namely to give up his clerkship in the Ministry and devote himself entirely to music. The manner in which he accomplished this is highly characteristic of the man, and needs now to be told.

CHAPTER THREE

Hears Tristan *in Munich—Resigns from Ministry to take up music as a career—Prowess as a pianist—Plans, then abandons, work on an opera,* Les Muscadins—*Joins Lamoureux as secretary and chorus-master—Publishes* Dix pièces pittoresques *for piano.*

BY THE year 1880 the Wagner fever in France, if not yet at its height (this was to come a little later) was rapidly gaining momentum. More and more Frenchmen, not only musicians but writers and artists as well, were making the pilgrimage to Bayreuth, and among the musicians who, like Saint-Saëns, Gounod, Rossini, Berlioz and others, had given their support, ever since the notorious *Tannhäuser première* in Paris in 1861, to this 'new' music, it was Henri Duparc who was one of the German master's most fervent admirers.[1] Duparc was also a close personal friend of Chabrier, and it was his insistence that the latter should accompany him to Munich in the summer of 1879 to hear *Tristan* that led to Chabrier's taking the decisive step which was to change the whole course of his career. From now on he would no longer merely be a musically gifted *rond de cuir* but a full-time professional composer.

It started with a simple request for leave of absence from the office for a few days contained in a letter so delightfully candid and disarming in its sincerity that it is worth reproducing here in full. (The reason the letter is addressed to M. Gustave Desjardins, who was Chabrier's *chef de bureau* and not to Pelletier, the *sous-chef*, who was his immediate superior, is that Chabrier knew that Desjardins was a great lover of music and more likely to be sympathetic to his request for leave.)

A M. Gustave Desjardins   [1880]

Monsieur,

Having some private business to attend to in Bordeaux, I would be very grateful if you would be good enough to grant me leave of absence for the three days that will be necessary to settle my affairs.

What I have just written is for my file! And now, since I never tell lies and perhaps for that reason have always enjoyed the confidence of my superiors, I must confess to you the real reason for my request: I have no intention of going to Bordeaux; but for the last ten years I have been longing to see Wagner's *Tristan and Isolde*. You can only see it in Germany, and next Sunday this great masterpiece will be given in Munich. I could wait no longer, and today I dashed off to get a *laissez-passer* as far as Avricourt which today, alas!, is our frontier. I have got it, and the rest of my expenses will be covered by the articles I intend to scribble for *Le Temps* or for *Le Petit Journal*.

That, Sir, is my crime; I'll confess it to you, but not to Pelletier, who mustn't know anything about it! I beg you to pardon this administrative escapade and to count on my devoted services. I shall be in my office on Wednesday morning at the latest.

Respectfully yours,

Emmanuel Chabrier.

Happily M. Desjardins gave his consent, and for an account of the effect which his first hearing of *Tristan* had upon Chabrier we must turn to a letter from Henri Duparc to René Martineau (one of Chabrier's biographers), which gives us a valuable insight into Chabrier's extreme sensibility where music was concerned, while providing direct evidence that it was the revelation he received at Munich that made him finally decide to devote himself entirely to music and sever all connections with the bureaucratic life:

. . . Emotion for him was, as it were, the *raison d'être* of music; he regarded as practically useless a purely cerebral art which may astonish but arouses no emotion. (This, perhaps, is one of the reasons why we have been such close friends, for I have always had the same ideas myself.) Convinc-

ing evidence of this attitude to music is revealed, almost
instinctively and in a curious way, in a score which I had
lent him to follow the performance from in the theatre in
which he had underlined all the emotional passages from
beginning to end. You can have no idea of what it meant to
him to be hearing *Tristan*, which he didn't know then, and
was almost afraid to get to know, as if some internal voice
was warning him that it was going to change his whole life.
There had been some very fine performances in Munich, and
I had been to hear the first; it was on a Sunday, and I was so
excited that I went back to Paris to persuade a few friends to
come for the second performance the following Sunday. One
of these friends was Chabrier, whom I went to see at his Ministry. He hesitated a long time, and raised a lot of objections;
but it seems I was able to persuade him, and at last he
promised to come along with us. Everyone was delighted,
because that meant that the journey would be amusing. . . .
He was so overcome (by the opera) that, although usually so
gay and cheerful, he left us after the performance and shut
himself up in his room. You know he didn't at that time
intend to devote himself to music entirely; *Tristan* made him
realize his true vocation, and on his return from Munich he
had made his decision.

Vincent d'Indy was a member of the party on this occasion, and
sat near Chabrier at the Opera in Munich; and many years later,
long after Chabrier's death, he told the following story:

The Prelude was about to begin, and silence and darkness
reigned in the theatre when we heard quite near us what
sounded like someone trying to stifle a hiccough . . . it was
Chabrier sobbing. . . . The person sitting next to him turned
round to inquire whether he was feeling ill, and our good
Chabrier replied, between two sobs: 'I know it's stupid, but
I can't help it . . . I've been waiting for ten years of my life for
that *A* on the 'cellos. . . .'

So much for the legend of a Chabrier, half peasant, half boule-vardier, romping his way through music, brash and extrovert, writing frothy operettas or noisy pieces for the orchestra. His essential humility and reverence for music are revealed in the words he uttered on leaving the opera-house in Munich on that fateful occasion: 'There's music there for a hundred years; he hasn't left us chaps anything to do. Who would dare?'

In the event, of course, this prophecy, inspired by what had been for Chabrier an overwhelming emotional and aesthetic experience and the revelation of what seemed to him at the time to be the *ne plus ultra* in music, was proved untrue; despite the influence of Wagner, there was already in being in France the nucleus of a breakaway movement headed by Fauré, Ravel and Debussy. Moreover, although it is true that it was Wagner's impact which, so to speak, sparked off Chabrier's latent creative genius and launched him on his career, all his best music, it is important to note, despite *Gwendoline*, is essentially French in spirit and wholly free from Wagner's influence. All his con-temporaries were agreed on this point, from César Franck to Ravel (did not the Franckist Pierre de Bréville call him 'le maître si clair et si français'?), and later observers, like Stravinsky and Koechlin, have, as we have seen, stressed this aspect of Chabrier's art.

The revelation of Munich was in the summer of 1880, but it was apparently not until November of that year that Chabrier finally handed in his resignation from the Ministry. He was now about to enter on the most productive period of his whole career, although he was only to live for another fourteen years. He was living now with his wife at 23 rue Mosnier (now rue de Berne) and had as a neighbour his great friend Edouard Manet, whose studio overlooked this street; and the painter was one of the 'regulars' at the gatherings which were held in the Chabriers' flat, the others being Duparc, Chausson, de Bréville, d'Indy, Messager and Saint-Saëns. Other frequent visitors were Charles Lecocq and two great personal friends of Emmanuel, Paul Lacome d'Estalenx and Edouard Moullé.[2]

At these gatherings music would be made in which everyone took part, some serious, some more frivolous, as when Saint-Saëns, for example, would delight the company by singing and playing with passionate fervour the role of Marguerite from Gounod's *Faust*, or someone would perform on an extraordinary organ with weird stops that imitated all sorts of sounds, including drums and cannon. But it was Chabrier himself who was the star on these occasions, dazzling his audience by his fantastic piano playing which all who heard it agreed was something quite unique—both as a spectacle and a musical experience. We have already mentioned the well-known caricatural portrait of Chabrier at the piano by his friend Edouard Detaille and Alfred Bruneau's description of his playing (page 6). Here is another vivid impression by an anonymous writer that appeared in the newspaper *Gil Blas* shortly after Chabrier's death, quoted by Yvonne Tiénot (1965):

> There was something clown-like and extravagant in his manner and method of playing which was both exciting and disconcerting. He would pound the piano with his hands, his elbows, his forehead, his stomach and his feet, extract from it the most fantastic sounds, attacking it like a whirlwind, forcing it to give out the most piercing clamour and only letting it go when the unfortunate instrument had no voice left and was staggering on its feet like a drunken man.

Another painter friend of Chabrier was Auguste Renoir, whose wife, an amateur pianist herself, has also, in her son's book, recorded her impressions of the composer's piano playing:

> Friends complimented me on my playing. Renoir made me read some of Schumann's melodies at sight. He had known Mme Schumann well before the war of 1870. Then one day Chabrier came; and he played his *España* for me. It sounded as if a hurricane had been let loose. He pounded and pounded the keyboard. It was summertime. The window was open.

While he was playing I happened to look into the street. It was full of people, and they were listening, fascinated. When Chabrier reached the last crashing chords, I swore to myself that I would never touch the piano again. An amateur playing is really ridiculous. Like the people who, just because they know Renoir, want to take up painting. How can they? Besides, Chabrier had broken several strings and put the piano out of action.

This story complements an anecdote told by Hugues Imbert relating to the famous musical evenings in the rue Mosnier:

It was springtime, and the windows of the little *entresol* in the rue Mosnier were wide open, and in consequence a little crowd assembled outside to listen to the stream of music that floated out. People used to clap and applaud, and one evening someone stepped out and made a little speech that was very apposite, saying: 'If I were your landlord I should be so pleased to have you for my tenant that I would offer you your lodging for nothing!'

Finally Edouard Schneider's account (1922) of Chabrier's prowess when improvising at the piano:

At the famous Auvergnat club in Paris, *La Soupe aux choux*, Chabrier was always greeted enthusiastically. We loved to hear him do one of his legendary improvisations. Someone would show him a newspaper with the description of some crime or accident and immediately he would start to sing it at the piano. If it was a crime he would dramatize it and create an atmosphere of terror—first suspense, and then you would hear the gendarmes' galloping horses. The criminal is arrested to the strains of a funeral march, and as the article ended with the words, 'the vindictive public will now be satisfied', Chabrier exclaimed: 'Now you'll see just how pleased the vindictive public was,' and the piano broke into a wild jig. . . .

But if these were Chabrier's distractions, he had no intention of wasting the extra time he now had at his disposal since he had freed himself from his duties as a civil servant. The work he now had on the stocks was a project for a four-act opera based on a novel by Jules Clarétie (1840–1913) entitled *Les Muscadins* (the name given to the young Royalist dandies of 1793 who were perfumed with musk and armed with enormous canes) from which a libretto had been prepared by the poet Armand Silvestre (1837–1901). This occupied him on and off for some years, even while he was engaged on what he regarded as his *magnum opus*, the opera *Gwendoline*, as can be seen from the following letter to his friend Edouard Moullé:

> For the moment I am working quietly at *Les Muscadins*. No more fairy stories or weird rhythms here; it's drama *à la* Dumas *père*; it's got to reflect the France of those days, and it's not easy to find the right colour for this. It's no longer the country of Make-believe where I like to dream and discover rhythms; no goblins, or anything like that—only patriots and chauvinistic songs and square-cut phrases; with my horror of banality you can imagine how complicated it all is. The subject suits me, above all because I see in it a speedy realization of my desire to be performed; in the highest circles the period will attract attention; it hasn't been done before; I'm certain I've a good chance of succeeding, but of course the kind of music that's called for here isn't so much up my street as *Gwendoline* or other works of a poetic nature. Well, we shall see. . . .

In the end, however, Chabrier became discouraged and the work was never finished. In fact, he only wrote four scenes, and they were incomplete; but on the MS. of one of them Chabrier had written: 'One of the best things I have ever done; d'Indy complimented me on it.' Nevertheless Mme Chabrier told a reporter, when her husband was a very sick man in the last year of his life, that he didn't like the work and had tried to destroy it.

Although *Les Muscadins* went to join the other 'might-have-beens', it is clear that Chabrier had given it a lot of thought—further evidence, if evidence be needed, of the serious and conscientious way in which he approached any new work before coming to grips with it.

The year 1881, his first year of freedom following his resignation from the Ministry, was in more ways than one an important one for Chabrier and a turning point in his career. Not only was it the year in which he published his *Dix pièces pittoresques* for piano, one of the works by which he will always be remembered, and which won for him the praise and admiration of all his fellow musicians; it was also in this year that he was invited by Charles Lamoureux (1834–99), the celebrated conductor and founder of the concerts bearing his name, to join his symphonic association, Les Nouveaux Concerts, in the dual capacity of secretary and chorus-master. Lamoureux was an ardent Wagnerite and had done more than anyone to promote performances of Wagner's music in France. He knew and admired Chabrier's music, and had met him often at gatherings of the little clan of Wagner enthusiasts known as *Le Petit Bayreuth* already mentioned (*see* Chapter One, page 11) and made famous by Fantin-Latour's picture *Autour du piano* with Chabrier seated at the instrument. A few years after his appointment Chabrier was entrusted with the supervision of rehearsals for the first two concert performances in France of *Tristan and Isolde* (1884–5), an historic event, and a task which must have been very much to his liking. This association with Lamoureux put Chabrier in the forefront of musical activities in Paris, and also in a privileged position so far as securing first performances of his own works was concerned, since Lamoureux thought highly of him and was always ready to do what he could to help his *protégé* in his career. He had been a member of the Société Nationale de musique (founded in 1871 by Saint-Saëns to promote French music in France with the collaboration of Alexis de Castillon (1838–73), César Franck, Fauré and Lalo) for some years already, and since his recent successes in the theatre was now no longer looked upon as an amateur by his contemporaries, but recognized as a composer of standing. Among his many musical friends Vincent d'Indy was one of the most devoted, and it was to Chabrier that he dedicated his first work for the piano, the *Poème des montagnes*, Op. 15. Whether or not his opinion of the work was invited, Chabrier wrote the following letter to his friend in which he does not hesitate to criticize where he feels criticism was called for:

Thank you, my dear fellow, for sending me your *Poème des Mont* [*sic*] which I find exquisite—especially the *Bruyères* [Heather] section, the whole of *Brouillard* [Mist] which would be delicious on the orchestra, and all the *Plein Air* [In the open] part—and finally the *A deux* [Together] and all the last pages. I'm not so keen on the *Danses rythmiques* [Rhythmic dances]; to begin with, the writing and especially the rhythms are certainly unusual, but these rhythms are broken up by the use of the thumb in the left hand and by too many effects one after another with so little regularity in their disorder that I've no time to be either astonished or charmed; the piece is over before I can form any opinion. Do I make myself clear? But isn't it perhaps I who am being a dunderhead? . . . In any case, you are a marvellous musician, with more skill than substance as yet, but inspired by the highest artistic ideals. Thank you again,

Affectionately,

Emmanuel.

It is now time to take a look at what was Chabrier's first important work for the piano, the *Dix pièces pittoresques* (a title probably not of his own, but of his friend Lacome's, choosing) which occupy a place apart in the literature of French piano music, so remarkable in the freshness of their inspiration and tranquil originality that after their first performance at a Société Nationale concert in Paris in 1888 César Franck was moved to exclaim to those around him: 'We have just heard something quite extraordinary. This music is a link between our own epoch and that of Couperin and Rameau.'

These pieces are indeed remarkable, and the fact that they are so rarely heard is more remarkable still. No doubt the idiom in which they are written is not 'fashionable' today, but any pianist musician enough to defy fashion and add them to his repertoire would not only be doing a service to his public but might well be enriched thereby himself. They are not all, of course, of equal merit, but the best among them are so good that they deserve to be heard more often. The astonishing thing about the *Ten Pieces* is that, while appearing superficially to be little more than rather high-class *salon* music they are seen on closer examination to be a veritable treasure-house of new and ingenious harmonic and rhythmic *trouvailles*, revealing a first-class musical imagination coupled with a rare sensitivity. Alfred Cortot and Francis Poulenc have both recorded in some detail their impression of these pieces in the studies from which we have already had occasion to quote; and it is interesting to see how, by and large, they are both impressed by the same qualities in the music. Speaking of No. 1 (*Paysage*) Poulenc remarks that this is not a 'romantic' landscape, but a joyous one, and should be played light-heartedly and with tenderness. For Cortot, it is more 'Malerei' than 'Empfindung', and lacking on the whole what he calls 'the element of contemplation'. No. 2 (*Mélancolie*) is the piece in which Ravel saw the musical counterpart of Manet's *Olympia*; and Poulenc reminds us that, being highly typical of Chabrier's style, it was evoked by Ravel in his *A la manière de . . .* Cortot sees in it 'a tender dialogue of question and answer . . .' and adds that the 'nostalgic charm and discreet perfection of this piece defy analysis'. No. 3 (*Tourbillon*) was used, as Poulenc points out, by Balanchine and Bérard in their ballet *Cotillon*. He describes it as a 'galop de salon, très 1880', and says that it must be played 'implacably'. It is frankly a *bravura* piece, showing Chabrier in one of his 'unbuttoned' moods—the kind of piece,

as Cortot suggests, that he might well have been playing in the
famous portrait-caricature by Detaille. In complete contrast is
No. 4 (*Sous-bois*) which Ravel especially admired, describing it as
one of the summits of Chabrier's *œuvre*, and remarkable for the
'extreme refinement of the harmonies. . . .' Cortot too calls
attention to the alternations of augmented fifths and common
chords, and describes the music as showing a rare 'poetic sensibility', evoking the murmur of trees in a forest under the summer
sun and an impression of 'ineffable monotony and beatitude'.
Over an unchanging *ostinato* figure in the bass, such melody as
there is is curiously fragmented in leaping arpeggios ornamented
with grace notes.

No. 5 (*Mauresque*) is a rather conventionally oriental dance, the
middle section of which, however, Poulenc points out, has an
echo in the *Forlane* in Ravel's *Tombeau de Couperin*. Cortot on the
other hand remarks that it recalls the *Nocturne* in Saint-Saëns's
Suite Algérienne. We come now to what Cortot calls 'the most
delicate jewel in the whole collection', No. 6 (*Idylle*). Pointing

out that it is written throughout in three real parts, he calls it
'musique adorable', full of grace and charm and musical subtlety.
For Poulenc too this piece is the gem of the collection, and he
describes the unforgettable impression it made upon him when he
heard it for the first time as a young man when he was living in a
world bounded by Stravinsky and Schoenberg, and thought at that
time, 'simpleton that I was—like many others today—that
Chabrier was a minor musician!' He had put a coin into a slot
machine at the Maison Pathé on the Grands Boulevards in Paris
to listen to a record by the famous pianist Edouard Risler (1873–
1929) not knowing what he was going to hear; and, he continues:
'Today I still tremble with emotion thinking of the miracle that
happened then; a new harmonic world opened up before me,
and my own music has never forgotten that first *baiser d'amour*. . . .'
Music so completely unselfconscious and uncontrived, so *natural*
that it seems almost like a sound in nature, is a rarity; but
Chabrier at his best has that quality which defies analysis, and it
is that which makes him so intriguing a figure—provided the
listener is tuned in on the same wave-length, an indispensable
condition.

About No. 7 (*Danse villageoise*) Cortot has more to say than
Poulenc, who merely lays down that it must be played straight-
forwardly, with no *rallentando* in the middle section. After observing
that the piece is a good example of Chabrier's 'robust musicality
with the flavour of his native province', Cortot makes the point
that the pre-Romantic minuet-scherzo form in which the piece
is cast suited Chabrier because this form implies repetition rather
than development, which was not his strong point. As for No. 8
(*Improvisation*), Cortot rightly observes that this piece reveals a
Schumannesque aspect of Chabrier's talent, and rather paradoxically, in spite of its title, shows more formal construction than
elsewhere, being, indeed, 'constructed like the first movement
of a sonata . . . a splendid page, rich in musical substance. . . .'
Poulenc contents himself with remarking that 'rarely is Chabrier
so romantic. . . .'

Marked '*fantasque et très passionné*' it is remarkable for its bold progressions and the brilliance of the piano writing. No. 9 (*Menuet pompeux*) was orchestrated by Ravel at the end of his life, and Poulenc, after suggesting that Ravel was inspired by it in his early *Menuet antique*, declares that this piece is the key work behind many pages of Debussy and Ravel. Cortot, less enthusiastic, speaks of the Minuet's 'popular accents', and opines that it 'gives the impression of a rather mannered sentimentality'. Finally No. 10 (*Scherzo-Valse*) according to Cortot 'justifies its popularity by its musical *franchise*, picturesque atmosphere and full-blooded, spicy accents'. Poulenc merely remarks that it should not be played too fast; the Trio in rustic style and rather more heavily.

The names given to the various pieces and the overall title of *Picturesque* are unfortunate in so far as they suggest that Chabrier attached any importance to 'literary' ideas in music, or was in fact interested in any extra-musical associations when composing. No more than the Impressionist painters, for whom atmosphere and sensuous qualities were more important than 'subjects', was Chabrier concerned with intellectual conceptions; and Delage (1963*a*) has drawn attention to a theory advanced by Paul Valéry, in his *Triomphe de Manet*, to the effect that the general aesthetic orientation of Chabrier, Manet and Baudelaire was basically the same because

> they do not wish to speculate on 'sentiment', or introduce 'ideas' without having skilfully and subtly organized 'sensation'. They aim at, in a word, and succeed in achieving, the supreme object of all art—charm—a term which I employ here in its fullest sense.

This means, of course, as the writer proceeds to explain, that

> they are not interested in a hierarchy of *genres*, but treat with equal seriousness any subject whether frivolous, familiar or

humorous, or seemingly of a more noble or elevated character—
an attitude which enables them to avoid the pseudo-sublime
as well as pedantry and that eloquence whose neck Verlaine
recommended all true poets to lose no time in wringing. And
so, just as a barmaid, a stick of asparagus or a woman pulling
on her stockings provided Manet with subjects for by no means
insignificant pictures, so did Chabrier raise to the level of
great art *opera-buffas*, romances, or short pieces for the piano.

In any case, the *Dix pièces pittoresques* must be considered one
of his most important and revealing small-scale works, preparing
the way, as it were, for his first major orchestral work *España*,
which might never have been written had not Lamoureux, for
whom Chabrier was now happily working, encouraged him to
undertake in the summer and autumn of 1882 the voyage
through Spain which was to prove such an important turning
point in his career.

CHAPTER FOUR

Travels in Spain and writes España, *his first big success—At country retreat in Touraine composes* Trois *valses romantiques for two pianos—Relations with Vincent d'Indy.*

THE CHABRIERS (Emmanuel and his wife) were in Spain from July to December 1882 and seem to have made a very comprehensive tour of the Peninsula, visiting San Sebastian, Burgos, Avila, Toledo, Seville, Granada, Malaga, Cadiz, Cordoba, Valencia, Saragossa and Barcelona. Some of his best letters were written during this tour, full of humour, keen observation and a frankly expressed delight in everything he saw and heard conveyed in that picturesque and lively language which, no less than his music, was an essential part of the man. The letters, indeed, are our chief source of information covering this period during which Chabrier was absorbing, as it were, as much of Spain in all its aspects, and especially its music, as he could, so that when the time came he would be fully primed with all the elements he needed to produce the work by which he will always be remembered, portraying vividly in sound the country to which, after France, he was most attached—*España.*

In his first letters, written from San Sebastian to his publishers and friends Enoch and Costallat, he has this to say about the fleas of Guipuzcoa which have been tormenting him since his arrival:

> The Spanish flea is above all patriotic and rarely emigrates. . . . Moreover, they have their national anthem, their *Marseillaise*, so to speak, in the form of a 3/4 in F major which a French composer, by name Berlioz, has introduced into his *Damnation of Faust*, as he also introduced the national air of Raccosky [*sic*]. As the province of Guipuzcoa is one of the coolest in the Peninsula the native fleas are inclined to feel

the cold and to seek warm and sheltered spots and, in consequence have a marked preference, which I well understand,
for the female body where they really feel at home. . . .

Then follow some harmless and typically Chabrierian *grivoiseries*
evoking the kind of happy hunting-ground most appreciated by
the fleas, with regard to which he adds:

I could tell you stories which would make the cover of Litolff's
edition blush.

Inevitably the Chabriers were anxious to see a bull-fight:

. . . Next Sunday, while with one hand you are watering your
garden and with the other blowing kisses to your wives, at
about four o'clock in the afternoon we shall all be at the
bull-ring. I've been dreaming about it for a week; it's unlikely
though that I shall take an active and direct part in the
proceedings as I had at first intended to do; my idea was
first to terrify the bull by presenting it with the manuscript
of the third act of *Les Muscadins*, and then to annihilate it by
singing the Third Waltz. My wife, however, is not in favour
of these rash actions, and says that I am only a dreamer. . . .

From Seville and Granada Chabrier wrote some of his most
memorable letters in a style which seems to show that he had a
genuine literary gift as well as keen and discerning ears and eyes.
It was at Seville, where he arrived in October, that he had his
first taste of flamenco dancing, and could not wait to convey his
impressions to his friends Enoch and Costallat:

Seville, 21 October 1882.

Eh bien! mes enfants—What an eyeful we're getting of
Andalusian behinds wiggling like frolicsome snakes! Every
night finds us at the *bailos flamencos* [*sic*], surrounded both of us
by *toreros* in lounge suits, black felt hats cleft down the
middle, jackets nipped in at the waist and tight trousers
revealing sinewy legs and finely modelled thighs. And all
around the gipsy women singing their *malagueñas* or dancing

the tango, and the manzanilla circulating from hand to hand
that everyone is forced to drink. Flashing eyes, flowers in
their lovely hair, shawls knotted at the waist, feet tapping
out an endless variety of rhythms, arms and hands quivering,
undulating bodies in ceaseless movement, dazzling smiles and
that admirable Sevillian behind moving in every direction
while the rest of the body remains motionless—and all the
while cries of 'Olé! Olé! ánda la Maria! ánda la Chiquita! Éso
es! Baile la Carmen, ánda! ánda! 'uttered by the other women
and the public! Meanwhile, the two solemn guitarists, puffing
their cigarettes, keep on strumming anything that goes in
3/4 (only the tango is in duple time). The cries of the women
excite the dancer who, at the end of her turn, becomes literally
intoxicated with her body—it's quite fantastic! Last night a
couple of painters accompanied us and made sketches, while
I was making notes of the music; we were surrounded by all
the dancers; the singers repeated their songs for me, and then
retired after warmly shaking our hands!! Then we all had to
drink out of the same glass—most hygienic! Anyway, we
were none of us any the worse for it next morning. All the
same, I don't quite see Mme E—— in that *galère*. . . . And to
think that we shall be leading this kind of life for a month,
until we get to Barcelona, after passing through Malaga,
Cadiz, Granada and Valencia! O my poor nerves! After
all, though, one must see what one can before kicking the
bucket—but, let me tell you, my friends, nobody has really
seen anything who hasn't witnessed the spectacle of two or
three Andalusian women undulating their behinds, keeping
time with each other and also with the *ánda! ánda!* exclamations and ceaseless handclappings; it's wonderful how they
clap instinctively *off-beat* in 3/4 time while the guitar steadily
keeps up the rhythm.

While the others are marking the down beat in each bar,
each more or less according to her fancy, this produces a most
curious amalgam of rhythms which, of course, I've been care-

fully noting down—but, O my friends, what have we let ourselves in for! Going round the cathedrals (magnificent), visiting museums, losing our way in the streets, seeing all there is to see, gobbling our meals and getting to bed at midnight—there are times when we seem to be going mad! On the slightest pretext we climb to the top of this blessed Giralda, from where you can see the finest panorama in the world; I know the name and the sound of all the church bells because the young bell-ringer is my friend; his sisters dance in a *boîte de nuit* and by day show visitors the cathedral. That's how it goes.

The streets are full of beggars who, with a cigarette between their lips, and looking very distinguished, ask you for alms; they don't say Thank-you, for it seems this is their prerogative. And all night long the *sereno* (night-watchman) patrols the streets with his staff and lantern, chanting in a loud voice: *Ava Maria purissima* etc. which means that all is quiet in the town and one can sleep peacefully. There's even a dance called the *Sereno*, in which the dancer imitates the said *sereno* and sings at the top of her voice *Ave Maria purissima* and waggles her behind. The theatres are detestable; society people don't go to dancing places; when they want this kind of thing the dancers go to their private houses. I'll write to you again in week. They're calling us for luncheon. Affectionate greetings,

Emmanuel.

In another letter to his friend Edouard Moullé, written from Granada, Chabrier goes into greater detail concerning his researches into the various regional dance-forms to be found in Spain, giving examples in musical notation of some typical rhythms.

I needn't tell you that I've noted down a quantity of things; only the tango in which the woman imitates with her behind the *tangage* [rolling] of a ship is in duple time; all the others without exception are either 3/4 (Seville) or 3/8 (Malaga and Cadiz). In the north it's different; here there are some curious 5/8s. The 2/4 of the tango is always in the *habanera* style. . . . The *sevillana* is different again—a 3/4 something like this (with castanets).

As for the *malagueñas*, they can hardly be written down; the melodic line has a kind of form and always ends on the dominant. The guitar plays a 3/8, and the man (when there is one), who is always seated at the guitarist's right hand, holds a stick between his legs and with it beats the 3/8 like this:

always syncopated. The women, meantime, instinctively syncopate the rhythms in a thousand different ways and manage while dancing to stamp an incredible number of rhythms with their feet, like this:

always with the heel—it's both rhythm and the dance at the same time. The tunes strummed by the guitar are not important; in any case they can't be heard above all the exclamations of 'Anda! Olé! Olé! la chiquilla! qué gracia! qué elegancia! Anda! Olé! la chiquirritita!'

In another letter (quoted by Pincherle, 1939), written in fluent but rough and ready Spanish to Charles Lamoureux, much of which is more or less a repetition of those quoted above, Chabrier for the first time alludes to the work he intends to compose on his return to Paris:

> . . . *una fantasia extraordinaria, muy española* . . . my rhythms, my tunes will arouse the whole audience to a feverish pitch of excitement; everyone will embrace his neighbour madly— and you, too, will be obliged to hug Dancla [leader of the orchestra] in your arms, so voluptuous will be my melodies. No more for the moment! Farewell, *hombre muy bravo*, farewell, chief of chiefs, farewell, enchanted baton, arm of iron, eyes of fire, indomitable spirit! . . .

In the event everything happened more or less as Chabrier had predicted; he did write his 'fantasia extraordinaria', and it was an instant success when Lamoureux conducted it at one of his Nouveaux Concerts on 4th November 1883—so much so, indeed, that it was encored at its first performance and had to be repeated the following Sunday and at several other concerts during the season. *España* had made Chabrier a celebrity overnight; it was played everywhere to packed audiences, and transcriptions and arrangements helped to spread its fame abroad. One of the most important of these was the arrangement for two pianos, eight hands, made by Lamoureux's son-in-law Camille Chevillard (1859–1923), another famous French conductor; while Emile Waldteufel (1837–1915), by turning it into a *Suite* of waltzes, no doubt increased its sales and popularity but at the cost of ruining its original character.

Parisian critics were almost unanimous in recognizing Chabrier's genius, and the composer must have felt especially honoured when so distinguished a scholar and authority on folk music as Louis Bourgault-Ducoudray (1840–1910) paid this tribute to him in an article published in *Le Ménéstrel* on 18th November 1883:

M. Emmanuel Chabrier, whose fantasy for orchestra *España* has just had such a decisive and legitimate success at the Nouveaux Concerts, belongs to that school of pioneer composers who copy Nature and are above all concerned to respect the truth. In listening to *España* one feels that he has been profoundly impressed by the popular songs and dances of Spain. . . . The way in which M. Chabrier has developed these themes of popular origin and inspiration effectively conveys the moods, now lively and impetuous, vociferous and stirring, or again full of languor and voluptuousness, so characteristic of Spanish song. The composer has invested them with the rich trappings of modern instrumentation, but without in any way depriving them of their primitive colour and popular accents. His orchestration is brilliant and full of colour, but free from eccentricities or abuses of any kind. Before leaving Spain M. Chabrier was wise to lay in a good provision of sunlight which he must have been pleased on his return to find on his compositional palette.

It is true that the themes and rhythms employed by Chabrier in *España* are in a sense authentic, notably the *jota* and the *malagueña*, and he was certainly one of the first, if not the first, French composer to write an important work in a genuinely Spanish idiom, thus inaugurating the vogue for Hispanically flavoured music which found its most perfect expression a quarter of a century later in such highly subtle and sophisticated works as Debussy's *Iberia* and Ravel's *Rapsodie espagnole*. As works of art these are, of course, immeasurably superior to *España*—a work which, in spite of a certain 'brashness', it is nevertheless impossible not to admire for its immense and refreshing vigour, exhilarating colour and brilliant orchestration. Originally written for the piano (it was Lamoureux who persuaded him to orchestrate it) it was one of Chabrier's favourite battle-horses on which he exercised his extraordinary gifts as a pianist; and this account in *Le Radical*, 11th January 1911 (Tiénot), from one who was privileged to hear him on one such occasion, is worth quoting:

> I shall never forget the day when, in the office of his publishers Enoch and Costallat, he consented to play for me— for me alone—this superb rhapsody. The contest was a terrible one; it was the piano that succumbed! The keys groaned, the strings twanged; the pedals bounced; the woodwork cracked while, with a smile on his lips, eyes sparkling and with beads of perspiration on his forehead, the master, like an infuriated bull let loose into the arena, attacked the instrument madly, with arms and elbows flying, until the keyboard, half de- molished, groaned in agony under his stubby fingers. It was both comic and sublime. After twenty-five years I can still see myself struck dumb with emotion in a corner of that horrible dark room which the flame of Chabrier's genius filled for a few minutes with light and beauty.

After the success of *España* Chabrier was now assured of his place among the leading French composers of his generation, and the stigma of being merely a 'gifted amateur' which had pursued

him for so long was now a thing of the past. It must be said in
fairness, however, that it was only in France that the work was
universally acclaimed; it was not a success in Germany, and still
less in Spain, where it was looked upon as being more than a
little bogus. This judgment, though harsh, is understandable,
for to a Spaniard familiar with the melodies and rhythms of his
native provinces it must have sounded rather as, say, a French
version of *Brigg Fair* might sound to an English folk-music
connoisseur. Francis Poulenc recalls Erik Satie's parody of
Chabrier in his own *Españana* (*Croquis et agaceries d'un gros bonhomme
en bois*) under the heading 'Plaza Clichy', which underlines
exactly the approach which made Chabrier's music unintelligible
to Spaniards—because it was too French. Just as Diaghilev once
said of Ravel's *La Valse* that it 'was not a ballet but the portrait
of a ballet', so, Poulenc observes, was Chabrier's *España* 'a
portrait of Spanish music by a painter of genius'. He does not
deny that it smacks a little of the Parisian 'grand magasin', but
thinks it is precisely that which gives it its special flavour. As
for Chabrier himself, anticipating Ravel's equally modest and
laconic description of his *Bolero* as a piece 'unfortunately devoid
of music', he liked to refer to *España* as 'a piece in F and nothing
more'. Nevertheless, from the point of view of orchestration
alone, *España*, no less than *Bolero*, is in its way a *tour de force*, and
in 1883 nothing quite like it had been heard before. As for the
famous trombone passage, which is pure Chabrier owing nothing
to Spain—

—Poulenc (1961) very pertinently observes that Stravinsky, albeit
unconsciously, may well have had this in mind when he wrote
in *Petruchka* a strikingly similar phrase:

1883 was a productive year for Chabrier, for hardly was the ink dry on his score of *España* than he had begun work on another important composition, highly characteristic and one of the most immediately attractive of all his works, the *Trois Valses Romantiques* for two pianos. Ravel, while still a student at the Conservatoire, had discovered and been fascinated by the *Trois Valses*, and had the honour of playing them to the composer a few years before his death with his young friend the pianist Ricardo Viñes, who was later to be so closely associated with the *avant-garde* movement in French music. The Waltzes were given their first public performance at the Société Nationale de Musique on 15th December 1883 with André Messager and the composer as soloists, and were an instant success. The piano writing is more orchestral than was customary at that time, and the style freer, much more spontaneous and even 'popular' in tone, bearing no signs of the scholasticism characteristic of d'Indy or Saint-Saëns. Cortot (1948) classes the *Valses romantiques* with the *Bourrée fantasque* as being the two most important of Chabrier's works for the piano and remarks on what he calls their 'surprising freedom of invention' and the way in which the skilful and ingenious piano writing is enhanced by the 'continuous dialogue between the two instruments and the resourcefulness displayed in the continuous exchange of ideas'. Poulenc comments on their 'melodic invention' and 'extraordinary pianistic and harmonic ingenuity' and suggests that in performance the sound quality should have the sort of sensuality that one feels in Renoir's picture *Fillettes au piano*.

Tender and passionate in turn, the Waltzes are immensely evocative, at one moment conjuring up visions of the ballroom with snatches of conventional, even banal, waltz tunes, at another storming the heights with extended *bravura* passages full of rhythmic and harmonic audacities and ingenious pianistic effects, with all the time in the background more than a hint of satirical humour to leaven the sheer high animal spirits of these delightful pieces which deserve a permanent place in the somewhat limited repertoire for two pianos. Chabrier composed them in a thoroughly contented frame of mind during his first summer at the country house in Touraine which his mother-in-law, Mme Dejean, had rented so as to provide him with a retreat to which he could escape from the turmoil of Paris and work in peace at least for a part of the year. In fact he formed the habit of retiring to La Membrolle-sur-Choisille, a small locality in the neighbourhood of Tours, from round about Easter until October; and though his wife and the children usually spent only the summer months at the villa, the faithful Nanine was with him all the time. Chabrier was essentially a family man, and a large proportion of his letters are written to his wife, to Nanine or to his sons. To his wife he describes in detail his daily routine and his delight in his new surroundings, and the following letter (quoted by Tiénot from the *Revue S.I.M.*) is typical of his affectionate nature and attachment to his family:

My dear good wife,

Your tender letter of yesterday morning gave me enormous pleasure; I read it and re-read it thirty times. These are the letters I like and, what's more, the letters I believe I deserve. But you don't tell me anything about our Marcel [the elder boy]; he's always out when you write to me; do arrange for him to be there when you have finished your letter. I'd like you to take his hand in yours and let him trace a few lines which, dictated by the mother and understood by the son, would go straight to the father's heart. Our Marcel would understand very well that he was writing to his old Dad, and would be remembering me while you were holding his hand. Despite the artificiality of this procedure, he would be thinking of me all the time, and one can't ask or expect more from him than that. . . . It's only for you all, and through you, that I live. . . .

The *Trois Valses* were thus, in a sense, the first fruits of his vacation in the country, and he wrote them spontaneously and

not this time for a commission, as he explains in a letter to his
great friend Paul Lacome:

> I'm writing some pieces for piano four hands; what for?
> you'll ask. I'm damned if I know, my poor d'Estalenx; it's
> idiotic, I know that, and the E's [Enochs] certainly won't
> want them—this one will be too long (never too short, of
> course), the other too difficult—or else it wouldn't be prac-
> tical. . . . That's the kind of life I lead. But no time was lost
> over the third Waltz; Baudon took it after he'd only been
> here five minutes. And, you know, I've an idea they may sell
> well. There's not much music for two pianos, and the young
> ladies who play the piano seriously (I don't need to tell you
> they're generally very plain) are bound to ask for them. But
> when they've read them perhaps they won't be so keen.[1]

Chabrier loved jokes and puns and riddles, and the acrostic
postcard he sent to his publishers to tell them the Third Waltz
was finished is typical:

Oiseau qui se pare des plumes du paon (geai)	= J'ai
[Bird dressed up in peacock's feather (Jay)]	
Qualification de la nommée Carabosse (fée)	= fait
[Nature of female named Carabosse (fairy)]	
Note de la gamme (la)	= la
[Note in sol-fa scale (La)]	
Oùsqu'il y avait un cheval de bois (Troie)	= troi-
[Place where there was a wooden horse (Troy)]	
Peintre ordinaire de la Place St Marc, Venise	= Ziem
[Well-known painter of St Mark's, Venice (Ziem)]	
Eau de table	= Vals
[Mineral water (Eau de Vals)]	

The *Three Waltzes* are far from easy and make considerable
demands on the pianists' technique; and, as we have seen,
Chabrier was very particular about the interpretation of his own

works, attaching great importance to exactitude, especially as regards tempo, rhythm and dynamic indications and, of course, a proper appreciation of the music's mood and content. Vincent d'Indy recalls how, when he was rehearsing the *Valses romantiques* with the composer, he was stopped in the middle of the first waltz by Chabrier exclaiming: 'Mais, mon petit, ce n'est pas ça du tout! . . . Tu joues ça comme si c'était de la musique de Membre de l'Institut!' (But, my dear fellow, that's not it at all! You are playing as if this was music by a Member of the Institute!) And then, d'Indy adds, there followed a wonderful lesson in interpretation, with cross accents, sudden outbursts, and almost inaudible *pianissimos*. . . . There is something piquant about the austere d'Indy, pillar of the *Schola Cantorum*, being thus lectured by the fantasist Chabrier, so long considered a mere 'amateur'; but there is no doubt that d'Indy was not only devoted to him but sincerely admired his music, unlike though it was to his own. For instance, he calls *l'Etoile* 'un petit chef-d'œuvre de musique drôle . . . as brilliant as the *Barber* and without any doubt more amusing and more musical than any operettas either before or since. . . . We find everywhere in his life as in his works examples of effusion, emotion, gentleness and tenderness without sentimentality, rare enough among our musicians today. . . . What is remarkable in Chabrier is that the qualities of tenderness and exuberance are so inextricably linked in his music that it would be impossible to tone down the one without harming the other. And it is that which, in my opinion, constitutes his undeniable originality.' As to Chabrier's prowess as a pianist, d'Indy pays him the highest compliments: 'He was an extraordinary pianist—in spite of his short arms and fat fingers he was capable of extremes of finesse and a command of expression such as very few pianists, with the possible exception of Liszt and Rubinstein, have ever equalled.' [2]

Another tribute from d'Indy took the form of an almost too sophisticated parody of Chabrier in the third book of his *Pour les enfants de tout âge*, Op. 74, published in 1920, which it is interesting to compare with Ravel's earlier pastiche (1914) in vol. ii of *A la manière de* . . ., a collection of parodies by Alfred Casella and Maurice Ravel. All this is further evidence, if evidence were needed, that Chabrier, however neglected he may be today, was a key figure, acknowledged and acclaimed by his contemporaries, in nineteenth-century French music; and our study of him is now entering upon the most productive and significant period in his comparatively short creative life.

Fragment of letter to Chabrier from d'Indy, 1892

CHAPTER FIVE

La Revue Wagnérienne—Genesis of Chabrier's first Grand Opera, Gwendoline—Production in Brussels successful but curtailed owing to Opera Director's insolvency—The work discussed—Creation of La Sulamite.

IT IS time now to examine in greater detail the extent and character of what I have called the 'Wagner fever' (*see* Chapter One, page 11, and Chapter Three, page 24) that had begun to spread rapidly in France (thus reversing the marked hostility aroused by his works at first) since the early eighteen-eighties. Confined to begin with to small groups of fanatics, quite as likely to be writers and poets and critics as professional musicians, or specialized coteries such as *Le Petit Bayreuth*, the movement rapidly gained ground, and by 1885 the Wagner cult had gained so many new adherents that it was felt the time had come for the foundation, with the backing of eminent artists and intellectuals, of a literary review which would be devoted to the discussion and dissemination of Wagner's theories concerning poetry, philosophy, drama and music. And so, on 8th February 1885, the *Revue Wagnérienne* came into being and appeared regularly every month for the next three years.

Its founder and director was the novelist and playwright Edouard Dujardin (1861–1949), inventor of the so-called *monologue intérieur* technique to be adopted later by twentieth-century novelists (e.g. Virginia Woolf and James Joyce), and enough of a 'man-about-town' to have been portrayed in the company of Yvette Guilbert on the famous poster by Toulouse-Lautrec, *Le Divan Japonais*. Another staunch supporter and patron of the *Revue Wagnérienne* was the notorious English Germanophil Houston Stewart Chamberlain (1855–1927), who married Wagner's daughter Eva and wrote copiously in support of Wagner and Germanic culture generally—activities which later earned for him the doubtful distinction of being Hitler's 'ideal Englishman'.

The *Revue* nevertheless had a list of contributors of quite extraordinary distinction, including almost every eminent name in the world of music and letters. The musicians included Liszt, Saint-Saëns, Alfred Bruneau, Charles Bordes (co-founder in 1894 with d'Indy and Guilmant of the famous *Schola Cantorum* where César Franck taught), Vincent d'Indy, Gabriel Fauré, Reynaldo Hahn, Gustave Samazeuilh, Maurice Emmanuel and Florent Schmitt; while among the poets and critics who collaborated were such notabilities as Gérard de Nerval, Mallarmé, J. K. Huysmans, Verlaine, Catulle Mendès and Villiers de l'Isle-Adam. The latter knew Wagner personally and had been received by him at Triebchen and was a regular Bayreuth pilgrim, as was also Catulle Mendès who was to be Chabrier's librettist in *Gwendoline* and other works, and was held by some to be responsible for diverting Chabrier from his natural bent as an essentially French composer of light or near-light music by persuading him to undertake grand operas on a heroic Wagnerian scale, a *genre* for which he was not temperamentally suited. His friend Vincent d'Indy even went so far as to declare that it was the 'serious operas' he had wrongly been persuaded to write that 'absorbed, without any benefit to art, the last creative forces of our poor friend and led him to the grave'.[1] d'Indy was not alone in holding these views, and Chabrier was aware of the distrust with which his allegedly 'Wagnerian' tendencies were regarded by many of his friends and admirers. He did not of course attempt to conceal his admiration for Wagner, but his reply to his critics was that this did not prevent him from being himself and writing the music he felt was his own and no one else's: 'J'écris de la musique *à moi, bien à moi*', he exclaimed on one occasion; '. . . for better or for worse, I want to belong to my own country, that is my first duty. . . . Wagner's music *belongs to him*, and one shouldn't steal from anyone, even if one is the poorer for it (but still honest).' And in point of fact, although Chabrier's style in

Gwendoline and some of his other large-scale works, such as *La Sulamite*, is occasionally somewhat inflated and would-be grandiose, there is nothing strictly 'Wagnerian' about it apart from a moderate use of *leit-motifs* and occasionally some strident orchestration.

The whole question of the influence of Wagner on the new French school of musicians who were coming to the fore in the eighteen-eighties is the subject of an article in the *Revue Wagnérienne* that appeared after the production of *Gwendoline* in 1886, from which the following extracts show clearly the climate of opinion prevailing at that time:

. . . And now already we see a new school of composers arising in France under the influence of Wagner headed by two who have been the heroes of this season—MM. Vincent d'Indy and Emmanuel Chabrier.

MM. d'Indy and Chabrier, and others with them, have, thanks to the theories and works of Wagner, learnt to repudiate the system of a poem in a rigid form, but they are still romantics at heart; that is to say, they are not exclusively concerned, as Wagner is, with expressing the growth and development of feelings and emotions [*développement sentimental*]; music for them is not the language of the new psychology—they are still virtuosos, and continue to embroider with variations situations with very slight and shallow emotional content. . . . As regards *Gwendoline*, half of it is sacrificed to descriptions, *divertissements* and serenades, while the other half is clearly an attempt at analysis, an attempt to follow through a series of sentiments, to express an emotion, to depict human nature—a timid and feeble attempt if compared to twenty bars of *Parsifal* or the *Missa Solemnis*, but a magnificent and admirable effort in these days when composers and public alike, under the influence of music such as Mendelssohn's, are complacent in their ignorance of theories, indifference to research of any kind and acceptance of a state of stagnation and trivial note-spinning.

Thus Chabrier gets a pat on the back for his opera as being a step in the right direction although evidently, in the opinion of the writer, not Wagnerian enough. The article is unsigned, and may not even have been the work of a musician; indeed, the odd and significant thing about the whole pro-Wagner movement in France at that time is that it was perhaps even more literary than musical; it was Wagner's *ideas* and theories quite as much as his music that appealed to most intellectuals. But Chabrier was not an intellectual, and it was the rich emotive content of Wagner's music that appealed to him far more than all his theories about opera and drama, art and politics, the art-work of the future and what Stravinsky (1936) has called 'this unseemly and sacrilegious conception of art as religion and the theatre as a temple'. Nevertheless the critics and some of his fellow composers were perhaps too ready to apply the Wagnerian label to any of Chabrier's more ambitious works, such as *Gwendoline*, without having really considered what this epithet implied. There were exceptions, and one of these was the composer and critic Ernest Reyer (1823–1909) whose opera *Sigurd* (produced at Covent Garden in 1884) had also been criticized as owing too much to Wagner's influence. What Reyer wrote (1886), defending Chabrier's originality and independence, was as follows:

He borrows from Wagner his superimposed chords, anticipations and prolongations; his frequently unprepared discords and every licence in the conduct of parts in contrary motion; he adopts the same harmonic systems with all their resulting rhythmical complications—all this I don't deny. It is also true that he makes use of descriptive tags and *leitmotifs*; but he leaves to the German innovator his lengthy narrations and interminable recitatives and, although he too constructs his work scene by scene, he does not disdain to append a descriptive label to each number, e.g. 'chorus', 'legend', 'duet', 'epithalamium', etc.

Reyer had also been one of the first, if not the only critic to

couple the names of Berlioz and Chabrier when he drew attention
to a certain similarity between the Overture to *Gwendoline* and
the Overture to the *Francs-juges*. Resemblances and analogies
between composers concerning manner, style, vocabulary, etc.,
and the resulting inevitable allegations of 'influence' can rarely
be factually established and often tend to be a matter of individual
opinion except, of course, in the case of glaring 'cribs' of which,
after all, there are not very many authentic examples. The impact
of Wagner on nineteenth-century music was bound to be terrific
and far-reaching until the reaction against it set in, and it was
felt in France as much as anywhere, at least until the turn of the
century. Consequently there were few composers who remained
altogether immune to the spell cast by the wizard of Bayreuth,
and Chabrier was no exception. Only in his case, so strong was
his own personality and so potent his innate and essential
'Frenchness' of temperament and artistic sensibility, that it
would have been just as impossible for him as it was for Debussy
to do more than experiment with one or two of Wagner's more
superficial technical procedures without getting involved in the
labyrinth of his basic aesthetic and philosophical theories. At
most, then, while it would be fair to say that there are in *Gwendoline* passages reminiscent of, for example, *The Flying Dutchman*
(perhaps difficult to avoid where sailors and the sea are concerned),
and some highly coloured purple patches, the opera as a whole
is definitely not Wagnerian in the sense of being either *durch-
komponiert* or abounding in declamatory passages, but is on the
contrary essentially lyrical and romantic in character. Indeed, it
contains passages which seem to foreshadow Debussy (as Poulenc
for one has pointed out) rather than recall Wagner, and the idiom
throughout is far more French than German.

   Chabrier knew very well the kind of criticism to which he
would be subjected with regard to *Gwendoline*, and in an interesting letter to his friend Edouard Moullé, written while he was
still working at his opera, he to some extent forestalled it.

   I quite agree with you: *Gwendoline* is a kind of musical

Liebig; it's too compact; one ought to take a cube and dilute it, then shake well before serving. But I have no ambitions in writing it, nor am I in any immediate hurry; I don't believe it will ever be performed; what I'm doing is to make sketches, as painters do and then hang them up in a corner of the studio telling themselves that that'll be a fine picture one day! As to *Gwendoline* being a flop, it will be one in a big way, but I'm certainly going to risk it. Opera librettos are always terrible; look at the 'book' for *Le Roi de Lahore*, it's enough to make you vomit, and the same goes for *William Tell*, but it's played all the same; *William Tell* has even been a success. . . . *Gwendoline* I think would be something of a curiosity and in a way *opportune*; there'll be a lot of speechifying over its coffin; it certainly won't be buried ignominiously and in silence; in any case the work isn't finished yet, and the poem will have sooner or later to be altered.

In another letter, written about the same time to his publisher Costallat, after admitting that he, like Lalo and even Franck, is certainly looked upon as *vieux jeu* by the younger generation, Chabrier adds: 'I'll go further; I believe that they sincerely think Wagner is worn threadbare already. But they are all writing *the same kind of music* which could have been signed by any one of them, no matter which one; it all comes out of the same stable. It's the sort of music they want to put everything into, but there's nothing there.' Then, after expressing his admiration and affection for Weber and Berlioz (especially *Oberon* and *The Damnation*, *Romeo* and *l'Enfance du Christ*), Chabrier makes it clear he is not prepared to swallow everything in Wagner. Refuting the idea that there is a lack of *unity* in Berlioz, or if there is, that it is better than being boring, he goes on: 'For the sake of unity, I was going to say uniformity, there are in Wagner quarters of an hour of music, or rather of bare narration, every minute of which must seem to any sincere person, devoid of prejudice or fanaticism, as long as a century. . . .' And once again Chabrier re-asserts his artistic credo: 'For my part, my first concern is to do what pleases me while trying above all to express my personality; and my second is not to be a bore. . . .' We can see now why he was not afraid to write his famous *Quadrille* for the piano duet, *Souvenirs de Munich*, parodying themes from his beloved *Tristan*. All this is further proof of Chabrier's absolute independence and contempt for fashion, and amounts to an intelligent appraisal of the situation as he saw it, especially so far as opera and operatic fashions were the concerned. He obviously had no illusions as to inadequacy of most contemporary librettos, yet he himself was never particularly well served by his librettists, and his choice of Catulle Mendès as his collaborator in his first 'grand' opera, and too ready acceptance of the banal and artificial subject and second-rate text which Mendès offered him, is surprising. The most probable explanation is that, having become involved with Mendès through his association with the Parnassian poets, Chabrier, in his haste to find at all costs a libretto for the full-scale opera he was now determined to write, turned naturally to the author with whom he was already in contact and who, he knew, had some experience in this kind of work.

Here, then, is a summary of the story of *Gwendoline*, opera in three acts, poem by Catulle Mendès, music by Emmanuel Chabrier, first performed at La Monnaie in Brussels on 10th April 1886. The action takes place in the eighth century on the coast of Britain, where a peaceful Saxon community is disturbed by an invasion of Danish pirates. Gwendoline, the daughter of the Saxons' overlord, the patriarch Armel, intercedes with the Danish chieftain Harald, who has already fallen in love with her, to save her father's life. He agrees, on condition that Armel consents to their marriage. Pretending to do so, Armel treacherously orders his men to massacre the Danes during the wedding festivities, and gives Gwendoline a dagger with which she is to kill Harald on their bridal night. She tries to persuade him to escape, but he refuses. Armel then attacks and mortally wounds Harald, while Gwendoline stabs herself with the dagger her father has given her; and the curtain falls as the lovers sing an impassioned duet.

The wonder is that, in spite of this banal and luridly theatrical plot, almost a caricature of 'grand opera' at his worst, Chabrier was able to invest it with real life and feeling, and his score contains some really fine music. The theme of the Danes, announced on the 'cellos in the Overture, has a fine sweep about it, and there is much to be admired in the rich and varied orchestra texture and very effective choral writing throughout. The composer departed from tradition in assigning the role of Harald to a baritone and that of old Armel, Gwendoline's father, to a tenor, and in his musical portraiture of the principals their characterization is well defined. All the music allotted to the Danes is studiedly fierce and barbaric; and there is an amusing story which Felix Mottl (1856–1911), who conducted the opera in Germany, used to tell, recalling how Chabrier, not wishing to interrupt rehearsals by making comments, had brought with him a score marked at all the relevant places with the one word 'brutal'. . . .

Act I. It is dawn when the curtain rises on the peaceful Saxon village by the sea, nestling (most improbably) amongst flowering shrubs and rhododendrons. The villagers emerge and hail the new day in insipid verse, of which the following is a specimen:

> L'air léger où l'aube naît,
> La grève où croît le genêt,
> D'azur limpide et de rose
> Tout s'arrose,
> Le jour naît.

> (The light sky where the dawn is breaking,
> The sea-shore where the broom is blossoming,
> All are bathed in glowing pink and blue,
> The day is dawning.)

But Gwendoline is already haunted by a presentiment that the terrible Danes are about to invade. Her father and her companions try to reassure her, but her vision of horror persists, and by the end of Scene ii has become a reality: the Danish pirates have disembarked and threaten the defenceless Saxons with their swords. Their ferocious leader Harald is about to strike Armel down when his daughter rushes between them in an effort to protect her father. Harald, dazzled by her beauty, drops his sword, dismisses everyone and remains alone with Gwendoline. Then in a long fourth scene which ends the act, the two lovers-to-be exchange confidences, Harald dwelling upon his ignorance of women and prowess as a warrior, while Gwendoline tries to soften him, first by offering him a crown of flowers, which he rejects, and then after singing for him at her spinning-wheel a ballad—

> Blonde aux yeux de pervenche
> Dites, que filez-vous?
> —Un drap de toile blanche
> Pour le lit de l'époux . . .

—ordering him to sit at the spinning-wheel and repeat what she has sung. Furious at being discovered by his soldiers in such a humiliating posture, he chases them away; then, seeing Armel approach, he asks him outright for his daughter's hand, and the act ends with the old man explaining to his followers his plan to massacre his visitors after the wedding ceremony. Gwendoline's 'Legend' in Scene ii describing the barbarians' dreadful aspect and cruel deeds, and evoking their war-cry 'Eheyo!' (shades of the Walkyries!), the Sword-song sung by the Danes in Scene iii and Gwendoline's 'Ballad' are the outstanding features of this very lively act.

After a *Prelude*, which Poulenc describes as 'idéal de tendresse', the first scene of Act II contains the famous *Epithalamium* in which the lovers, after obtaining Armel's blessing, sing an impassioned duet accompanied by the full chorus, at the end of which Armel surreptitiously gives Gwendoline a knife, telling her to kill Harald as soon as they are alone together. She tries to persuade him that he is in danger, but cannot give a reason for her fears, and as he becomes more and more ardent she joins him in an another passionate duet until they are interrupted by sounds of a struggle outside and cries of alarm as the Danes are attacked by the treacherous Saxons. Gwendoline gives Harald her knife, and he rushes out as the curtain falls. The short third act (which is logically a continuation of Act II and is sometimes performed as such) is ushered in by a stormy Introduction in which the theme of the Danes is prominent. Against a lurid background of burning ships in the harbour the Saxons pursue and cut down the invaders. Harald is attacked and, surrounded by the infuriated Saxons as he clings to a tree, is mortally wounded by Armel's sword. Gwendoline, seeing his plight, stabs herself in despair, and together, still standing upright, they sing a last impassioned duet:

> L'heure est venue de prendre vers le beau Walhalla
>   notre essor!
> Sur un fier cheval blanc je serai [sings Gwendoline]
>   dans la nue la Walkyrie au casque d'or!

To this somewhat melodramatic libretto Chabrier has composed some memorable music in which the lyrical fervour of the love scenes is matched in intensity by the stark and brutal realism of the scenes of violence and heroic braggadocio. Though one feels the subject is not ideally suited to Chabrier's particular type of genius, he rose magnificently to the occasion; and *Gwendoline* is an opera which, though scarcely conforming to the tastes of today, is yet as deserving of revival as many of the faded Italian mediocrities that are resurrected from time to time. It is scored for a large orchestra including bass clarinet and usual woodwind, horns in F and C, trumpets, trombones and tuba, '*pistons*' (probably cornets) in B flat, side drum, cymbals, triangle, two harps and usual strings. Harmonically the music is very advanced for its period, abounding in sevenths and ninths without preparation or resolution (foreshadowing Debussy and Ravel), bold semitonal clashes and abrupt and sometimes subtle modulations. The

following is a striking example of Chabrier's free and uninhibited
harmony:

Gwendoline was Chabrier's first really big work, and not unnaturally
he had been hoping that it would have its first performance at the
Paris Opéra. To his great disappointment it was turned down, but
fortunately for him the Director of La Monnaie in Brussels,
one Henri Verdhurt, who knew and admired his music (he had
probably heard extracts from *Gwendoline* when Lamoureux conducted them at his concerts in 1884 and 1885), decided to produce
the opera at his theatre less than a year following its completion
in June 1885. And so in September of that year we find Chabrier
writing to Verdhurt as follows (Pincherle, 1946):

My dear Director,

    Thank you for your affectionate letter which I received this
morning, just as I was about to write to you. Actually I had
the honour yesterday morning to play to M. Gevaert two-
thirds of my score, and he will be seeing you shortly to discuss
it.[2] He told me he would be leaving for Brussels tonight or

tomorrow morning, and I would be greatly obliged, my dear friend, if you could see him as soon as possible and let me know the result of your talk. . . .

In the rest of the letter Chabrier expresses surprise that he should be expected to supply orchestral parts, as he understood that the management of La Monnaie would be responsible for all copying that might be necessary. This was customary in most theatres, and neither he nor MM. Enoch, his publishers, were prepared to defray the cost which they felt should be borne by the theatre. We are not told what the final decision was, but the incident shows that Chabrier, the impulsive, unconventional Bohemian, also had a practical side to his character.

When it became known that *Gwendoline* was to have its *première* in Brussels, all Chabrier's friends rallied round and announced their intention of being present to lend him their support on the great occasion. Vincent d'Indy was delighted at his friend's success and was determined not to miss the first performance at La Monnaie, as the following letter shows (Pincherle, 1946):

Dear old friend,

I've given your messages to our friends. As for me, Thursday is impossible because I've got a concert that evening. But now *read carefully*: I'm determined to be there for your *première*— I've put off various things for that, and will arrive on Saturday at 2 p.m. with Cl. Blanc (the others must make their own arrangements, that has nothing to do with me); but for Blanc and myself you simply must have two seats—we will pay whatever is necessary. We will even pay M. Verdhurt if necessary, but it's essential that he should give or sell us two seats for Saturday evening—and see to it if possible that we are not in a box at the side at the top of the house. If by any chance your *première* was postponed and didn't take place on Saturday, it would be most annoying, because I should have to put off again things I've put off already; but in that case you would know about it on Thursday after the dress rehearsal. Send me

a wire immediately. I would also ask you to telegraph as
briefly as possible to let me know (a) whether Blanc and I can
count on our seats; (b) in what low-down establishment we
can find you at 2 o'clock on Saturday when we arrive in Brussels. Don't let's miss one another, above all, for we have to go
back on Sunday as I have business on Sunday morning. Now
hurry up with the telegram, and best greetings from your old
pal who's looking forward to hearing your Gwendoline give
tongue [gueuler].   Vincent d'Indy.

Gabriel Fauré also wrote to say he hoped to be present:

> I was in Brussels the other day and I saluted the façade of La
> Monnaie in honour of Gwendoline. You may be sure that
> unless I am unavoidably prevented I shall certainly be on the
> train with all the other friends when the great day arrives. I
> have heard the most glowing accounts of all the parts in your
> work I have not yet heard myself, so don't be nervous; every-
> thing is sure to go well, and we shall all be happy for you.
>
>   Affectionately,
>   your old
>   Gabriel Fauré.

Another fellow composer and friend of Chabrier's, Ernest Reyer,
also made a point of attending the first performance of Gwendoline,
and in a letter telling Chabrier that he was going as the representative of the Journal des Débats, he wrote: 'I anticipate a great
success and am very delighted at the prospect.'

The opera was duly produced at the Théâtre de la Monnaie on
10th April 1886, and was, as everyone had expected, an enormous
success. The public was enthusiastic, and the composer was called
twice before the curtain to acknowledge the applause. The leading
parts, Gwendoline, Harald and Armel, were played respectively
by Mlle Thuringer and MM. Bérardi and Engel; the conductor

was J. Dupont. The critics were unanimous in praising the work's vigour and originality, and many of them were indignant that a composer as distinguished as Emmanuel Chabrier should have remained for so long in comparative obscurity. Unfortunately on this occasion again (the reader will recall the fate of his earlier operetta *L'Etoile*) Chabrier was dogged by his habitual ill luck and, after only two performances, *Gwendoline* had to be withdrawn as the Director of La Monnaie had been declared bankrupt.

Having got so far on the road to success, this unforeseen setback was a great disappointment for Chabrier whose thoughts, as a result, turned naturally once more in the direction of the Paris Opéra. His friends rallied round and some two years later a complete audition of *Gwendoline*, with singers from the Opéra, was given privately in the *salons* of Princess de Scey-Montbéliard in the hope that this would lead to its acceptance by the Director of the Opéra. Fauré played the harmonium, Chabrier the piano, and d'Indy and Messager were in charge of the percussion. The conductor was Gabriel Marie. Unfortunately this performance did not produce the desired result, and it was not until December 1893 that *Gwendoline* was at last admitted to the Paris Opéra, after having had its first performance in France at Lyons in April of that year. But by this time Chabrier was a very sick man, suffering from the general paralysis from which he was to die the following year, and, though present in person, he was mentally incapable of grasping the full significance of this important event to which he had looked forward so eagerly for so many years. Indeed he seemed barely to be aware that he was listening to his own music, and would turn from time to time to his neighbour murmuring, 'C'est bien, c'est même très bien', and was bewildered when he was called upon to acknowledge the applause. This sad incident had an almost exact parallel in 1936 when Maurice Ravel, also suffering from an incurable condition which affected his brain, was taken to see a performance of his ballet *Daphnis et Chloë* and after the performance remarked to those around him: 'Mais il avait du talent, ce Ravel. . . .' And, like Chabrier, whose music he loved and to whom he always said he owed so much, within a year of hearing in very similar circumstances, but failing to recognize, one of his own best works, he too was overtaken by death.

It should be mentioned here that although seven years elapsed between the production of *Gwendoline* in Brussels and its first performance at the Paris Opéra in 1893, the work was successfully produced in several towns in Germany in the intervening years, thanks to the intervention of Chabrier's friend the Wagnerian tenor Ernest van Dyck (1861–1923) and the strong backing of the Austrian conductor Felix Mottl.[3] This important phase in Chabrier's career will be reviewed in greater detail in a subsequent chapter.[4] In the meantime, within a year of the premature demise of *Gwendoline* in Brussels, Chabrier was to score another triumph with the work which is perhaps his masterpiece, *Le Roi malgré lui*, an *opéra-comique* in three acts, produced at the Théâtre National de l'Opéra-Comique in Paris on 18th May 1887. This is the work which Ravel declared he would be prouder to have written than Wagner's *Ring*. In the interests of chronological order, however, it is necessary first to mention briefly here one of Chabrier's finest choral works, the *scène lyrique*, *La Sulamite*, a setting of a poem by Jean Richepin scored for mezzo-soprano, female chorus and orchestra. The text is based on extracts from *The Song of Songs*, and the work was performed for the first time at a Lamoureux concert in Paris on 15th March 1885. The composer considered it one of his best works, and in a letter to his publishers (quoted by Tiénot) he wrote:

> I am very attached to this work. It is difficult, but will perhaps be less so in ten or twenty years from now. There are sure to be some young 'new century-ites' who will say it's idiotic, but that's not a reason for doing nothing but philosophize. . . .

It does not seem to have made a very great impression at its first performance, but the composer and critic Alfred Bruneau (1857–1934), who was associated with Zola in many of his operas, of which the best known is *L'Attaque du Moulin*, and the author of a remarkable *Requiem* (which was produced by the Bach Choir under Sir Charles Stanford in London in 1896), wrote an enthusiastic notice in the *Revue Independante*, describing the work as 'a triumphant Hosanna, a sustained outpouring of passion formidable in its final paroxysm'. And, indeed, the work has a glowing intensity and strongly sensuous aura, unlike anything else in Chabrier's *œuvre*; while the writing for both voices and orchestra is singularly free and uninhibited, and enlivened by all kinds of harmonic subtleties and bold and original modulations. There are a number of high B flats and some disconcerting leaps in the solo part which are most unusual for their period, and for choral societies on the look-out for something outside the hackneyed vocal repertory *La Sulamite* might be well worth reviving. Chabrier re-orchestrated it in 1890, and it was revived by the Concerts Lamoureux in 1902 and again in 1909. In 1911 it was taken up by the Société des Concerts du Conservatoire, and performed as recently as March 1964 under the direction of D.-E. Inghelbrecht (*b*. 1880), the friend and trusted interpreter of Debussy and a lifelong admirer and champion of Chabrier's music. In this connection it is interesting to note that Debussy confided to the French critic and composer Gustave Samazeuilh (1877–1967) that he was greatly influenced by *La Sulamite* when he was writing *La Demoiselle élue*, especially the open-ing bars. The resemblance, or rather affinity, is indeed striking:

(a) Chabrier

(b) Debussy

It is time now to turn to the work to which Chabrier was to give all his attention in the year that followed the ill-starred production of *Gwendoline* in Brussels—the *opéra-comique* that was to bring him universal fame, *Le Roi malgré lui.*

CHAPTER SIX

Composition of Le Roi malgré lui—*Production at the Opéra-Comique cut short when theatre is destroyed by fire—Chabrier meets Felix Mottl in Karlsruhe where* Gwendoline *is performed for the first time in Germany and later in other German towns.*

IT IS a tribute to Chabrier's resilience and moral courage that though naturally deeply disappointed at the catastrophe which, through no fault of his own, had cut short the successful production of *Gwendoline* in Brussels, he immediately started to look about him for another subject on which to base an opera. For he was still convinced that it was in the lyric theatre that his talents would find their best expression. He did not have to wait long. An opportunity was soon offered him to compose an *opéra-comique*, this time on a libretto based on an old-fashioned comedy, originally produced at the Palais Royal in 1836 and entitled *Le Roi malgré lui*. The authors of the libretto were two rather obscure hack writers, Emile de Najac and Paul Burani, who it seems were not even good at their job, so that in the end Chabrier had to enlist the services of his friend Jean Richepin (1849–1926), who was a poet and dramatist of considerable distinction. Poulenc, who had access to the original MS. of the libretto and correspondence and notes relating thereto, makes it clear (1961) that Chabrier was not at all happy with the work of his librettists and had frequently to suggest alterations and make corrections himself. He found the text lacking in movement (on one page he had scribbled 'Avancez, avancez!') and often mal-adapted to musical requirements. On one folder containing the draft text Chabrier had written: 'We have here a bit of everything—a *bouillabaisse* of Najac and Burani cooked by Richepin and spiced by myself.' In the end it was Richepin who was entirely responsible for whole scenes in each of the opera's three acts; and sometimes Chabrier would suggest improvements even to Richepin,

who finally got tired of patching up other people's texts and left
it to the composer to tidy up the third act himself. And yet,
though once again badly served by his librettists, Chabrier,
thanks to the freshness, spontaneity, irresistible charm and
superb musicality of his score, was able to invest this rather
faded and artificial comedy with more than a semblance of real
life in which comedy, romance and genuine sentiment are skilfully blended. The story on which the piece is based, and from
which its title is derived, is a page of authentic history, for the
central character is none other than Henri de Valois, the future
Henri III of France, who was persuaded by his mother, Catherine
de Medici, much against his will, to accept the throne of Poland
at a time when it was customary in that country to choose for
their king a foreign prince. Around this historic theme the
authors embroidered an improbable imbroglio, of which the
following is a brief outline.

Henry is now King of Poland, but is homesick for his native
land. He learns that a conspiracy is afoot to overthrow him, of
which the ringleader is Count Laski, the Palatine, who had
supported the unsuccessful candidate for the throne, an Austrian
archduke. Henry sees in this plot a way of escape for himself and
decides to encourage it by pretending to be one of his own courtiers named Nangis and allowing the conspirators to believe that
Nangis is the king. He promises to help them to get rid of the
king, but things take an unexpected and unpleasant turn when
he learns that Laski has decided that the king must be killed.
Nangis, however, is having a love affair with Minka, a serf-
girl, who contrives his escape, and in the end Henry (who in
the meantime has discovered that Alexina, the wife of the
comic Court Chamberlain, Fritelli, is an old flame of his)
consents to remain on the throne of Poland, a 'king in spite of
himself'.

Chabrier tackled his new task with alacrity very soon after his
return from Brussels and completed it so quickly that by the
following spring (1887) it had been accepted and was put on at

the Opéra-Comique in Paris. That he had some misgivings about
the new opera and was worried about finishing it in time can be
seen from the following letter he wrote to Lacome in June 1886
from his country retreat in Touraine:

> . . . . I was delighted to get your letter . . . there was nothing
> in the newspapers or in the theatre or art world; time went by
> and I felt you were far away from this rotten old Paris where
> there's no place for us, as there is for the bourgeois, and where
> our wretched nerves, always on edge, are like nothing so much
> as a guitar in the hands of half a dozen raving madmen all
> plucking its strings at the same time. . . . I've been stagnating
> for I don't know how long; now it would seem that things
> are beginning to move—but not just yet; I've got three acts
> to do in three months—I can't do it. . . . You're left to
> moulder for fifteen years, and then everything's got to be done
> immediately without giving you time to swallow. You slave
> away, doing your best, and then one fine day it's a glorious flop
> and you're sitting on your backside for ten years. There's been
> so much talk about *Gwendoline* that if this comic opera I'm
> fabricating at the moment [*Le Roi*] is not a success then, old
> boy, I'm done for. . . . Anyway, I'm finishing the first act
> (vocal score); by 1st September I shall probably be through
> (still only vocal score). Then I shall have three acts to orches-
> trate, two *entr'actes* to write as well as an overture, revision,
> and then cutting (that won't take so long) and goodness know
> what else. . . . Oh, how I detest being pushed about!—but
> one thing I won't do is to make any concessions. . . . It won't
> be performed until I'm satisfied myself, when I've finished it
> after working conscientiously but not overworking—or else
> I'll send the whole thing to blazes and it won't be played at
> all. . . . If it's not good then there's nothing doing. *Everything*
> is a great effort for me; I haven't got what's called *facility*.
> However little I have to do I have to retreat to my den, and
> once there I feel as if I could never do a stroke. . . . As to this

piece I'm working at, it's got to be very gay and slick, and get
a lot of laughs. . . . All this is very worrying. Oh! well, we
shall see. . . .

As it turned out, he not only completed the opera in six months
but had every reason to be satisfied with it. For *Le Roi malgré lui*
is a masterpiece in its *genre*, a model of what good light music
should be. It also marks a date in the history of French music.
Not only is it full of delightful melodies, spirited and resource-
fully designed *ensembles* and all kinds of witty and humorously
dramatic touches: the actual musical idiom in which it is written
sets it in a class apart from all other French light operas of the
period, with their trite, well-worn clichés and unadventurous
harmonies. One can well understand why Ravel was so captivated
by this music and what it was that moved him to declare that 'la
première du *Roi malgré lui* a changé l'orientation de l'harmonie
française'. One sees what Roland-Manuel (1951) meant when he
wrote that 'Erik Satie's second *Sarabande* was the link that con-
nects Emmanuel Chabrier's *Le Roi malgré lui* with Debussy's
Pelléas et Mélisande'. For here for the first time we find harmonic
progressions that were absolutely new in French music at that
time, although later they were to become part of the normal
vocabulary of Debussy and Ravel—notably the introduction of
unprepared and unresolved chords of the seventh and ninth, such
as we find on the very first page of the overture to *Le Roi*:

This is, of course, one of the best known examples of this procedure, of which we find an echo in Satie's three *Sarabandes*

published in the same year (1887) but a few months later than the
first performance of *Le Roi:*

Second Sarabande

The opera is so full of entrancing music that it would be possible
to point to something especially beguiling on almost every page.
In the first act, for example, besides the lively choruses of soldiers
and courtiers, there is the exiled Henri's nostalgic evocation of
his homeland:

> Cher pays, pays du gai soleil
> Si loin de toi, quelle est ma souffrance!
> Je te vois dans le songe, au réveil,
> Toujours, partout, cher pays de France!
>
> (Dear fatherland, land of bright sunshine,
> How I suffer far from thee!—
> Always in my dreams and waking hours
> Everywhere I see thee, dear land of France!),

the duet sung by Minka and Henri in praise of Nangis, and the
amusing *Terzetto*, 'Douce surprise, ma beauté de Venise', in
which Alexina and Henri recall their romance in Venice to the
discomfiture of Fritelli, Alexina's comic husband, who sees the
whole thing as a 'triste surprise'. Chabrier is one of the few composers who can be witty in music as well as humorous, and tender
without being sentimental; and no composer lacking in these
qualities would have been able to produce a work of art out of

material so unpromising, to say the least, as the libretto of *Le Roi malgré lui*. This no doubt has been the chief obstacle to a long overdue revival in the theatre of this otherwise admirable work which to modern audiences is known only through concert performances of the famous *Fête Polonaise* that opens the second act, a superb *bravura* piece, exuberant and intoxicating in its compulsive rhythms and brilliant orchestration.

For some further comments on other memorable features in the opera let us turn now to a letter from Vincent d'Indy to Chabrier (quoted by Pincherle, 1946) conveying his impression after attending the dress rehearsal; the date is 17th May 1887:

> My dear old friend,
>
> I couldn't get round to shake hands with you after the rehearsal, but I want to tell you how delighted I was with your Monarch. It's got some absolutely exquisite things and —what I like better still—things that are absolutely new and that no one before you has ever done. The whole of the second act is absolutely ravishing, from the waltz which has all the old Chabrier *entrain* [*alla Chabriero vecchio*] down to the finale which will be enormously effective. The duet with the violin scales is charming (the chorus of soldiers comes off very well); and then there's my 'Tuer le roi, c'est chose grave', which I'm mad about. In a word, the whole of the second act gave me enormous pleasure. In the third there's a *trouvaille* as fine as anything I know in music because it touches the heart and is sincerely felt—and that is the '*nervoso-sentimentale*' piece where Minka welcomes her 'grand monsieur bleu'. That's something that bowled me over each time I heard it; 'c'est vraiment du bel art', and one is pleased to be the friend of someone who could feel that and express it. And now would you like to hear the 'buts'? I'm sure you would, we're too old friends to stand on ceremony. I personally can only see one musical 'but'—it's a big one and embarrassing—I mean Mézeray's [Cécile Mézeray, who sang Alexina] big aria in the

first act. It makes the first act drag, and though I'm not a great 'cutter', I wouldn't hesitate to cut this number; all our friends feel the same about it, and it's my sincere opinion. I'm quite happy with all the rest of the music.[1]

As for the other 'but', it's going to annoy you, but here goes . . . I don't understand the plot . . . there are too many doors and chapels [oratoires] where people go in and out, arriving when they ought to depart, or going away when they ought to stay where they are—I don't understand. . . . Carvalho [Director of State Theatres] must have messed it about a lot—his heavy hand is recognizable and hasn't helped matters at all. I oughtn't to be telling you all this the day before the première, but it's done now—tant pis, you won't be angry with me. Till tomorrow, then; but I won't be able to get there before the second act which I badly want to hear again, because I like it enormously. Tomorrow you're sure to have a big success and ' les camarades (les vrais)' will be as pleased as the public because this is real music.

Yours in haste,

(I felt I must write you a line before tomorrow) and amitiés de ton vieux camarade qui t'aime sincèrement,

Vincent d'Indy.

'This is real music'; d'Indy in four words has stressed the quality above all others that distinguishes almost everything that Chabrier wrote, and is nowhere more apparent than in this delightful and most unjustly neglected opera—which has everything that Offenbach has, plus an instinctive and innate musicality and classical purity that lift it on to a level of high art which the composer of La Belle Hélène perhaps never quite attained.

Chabrier makes considerable demands on his singers and expects his leading ladies to be able to sustain high A's for as much as three bars, and to soar on occasion to C in alt. It seems that his publishers were a little apprehensive on this account, for we find Chabrier writing to them as follows:

> I have just been reading again the third act (orchestra) of *Le Roi*. Nothing must be altered; the 'grand' duo *must not* be transposed in the full score; only the theme at the beginning is rather high, and after the entry of Nangis (if altered) it would lose all its *éclat*, especially in the 6/4 in C major. In the provinces or abroad short-winded sopranos are at liberty to transpose in the orchestra the passage in question; but I can't begin this piece in G minor and continue in C or in A. . . .

Then follow various suggestions as to who among his fellow composers can be trusted to correct the proofs, or rather to revise his own corrections, among those cited being Messager and d'Indy: 'It must be someone fresh and new, for at the moment I'm incapable of seeing anything clearly. . . .'

Chabrier must indeed have been feeling the strain of three or four months of intensive work, but his efforts were rewarded by the almost immediate acceptance of his opera by Carvalho, Director of the Opéra-Comique, and its production in that theatre on 18th May 1887 barely a year after the ill-fated production of *Gwendoline* in Brussels. *Le Roi malgré lui* was enthusiastically received, and a critic in *L'Evénement* described it as 'an important musical event likely to bring about a real revolution—a fruitful revolution—in the modern theatre'. Another wrote (in *La République*): 'The public seem to have been enchanted by M. Chabrier's music. This is not surprising for it is exquisite. Impossible to pick out the best numbers, for each one is better than the one before.'

Everything then seemed set fair for a long run—but once again Chabrier's habitual ill luck asserted itself and his highest hopes were dashed to the ground. For in the very first week, after only three performances of his opera, the theatre was totally destroyed by fire. And so for the third time in his career Chabrier's hopes for a big success in the theatre were disappointed through no fault of his own. In 1878 the run of his operetta *L'Etoile* was prematurely ended owing to financial difficulties, and again in 1886 the same fate overtook his big opera *Gwendoline*. And now the very theatre in which his latest offspring had been successfully launched was burnt to the ground just as his long-nourished ambition to be performed at the Paris Opéra-Comique looked as if it were at last about to be fulfilled. Fortunately the score of *Le Roi* was saved, and later in the year the opera was mounted again for eight performances in the old Théâtre Lyrique in the Place du Châtelet where the Opéra-Comique found temporary accommodation, and for another six the following year in the same theatre. These were the last performances to be given in Paris during the composer's lifetime, but in 1892, the year before he died, *Le Roi* was produced at the Capitole in Toulouse. There were revivals in Paris at the Opéra-Comique in 1929, 1937 and 1941 (Chabrier's centenary year), since when it appears to have dropped out of the repertory in France. In Germany, however, it was given in the composer's lifetime, much to his satisfaction, in Karlsruhe, Dresden and Munich in 1890, and in Cologne in 1891, sharing the honours with its predecessor *Gwendoline*, which between 1889 and 1891 had been acclaimed in Leipzig, Stuttgart and Düsseldorf in addition to the other towns mentioned above (with the exception of Cologne).

Chabrier in this way had now become for the first time an international figure in the world of music and was about to embark upon an entirely new phase in his career, which necessitated frequent visits to Germany. These visits led to new relationships of which the most important was his friendship with the distinguished Austrian conductor, Felix Mottl, who had made himself personally responsible for the production of Chabrier's operas in Germany.

To understand how this came about it is necessary to turn back for a moment to the time when Chabrier was working as Lamoureux's assistant and collaborating in the first concert performances

in France of Wagner's works (*see* Chapter Three). One of the
principal singers who took part in these performances was the
young Belgian tenor Ernest van Dyck, and despite the difference
in their ages (Chabrier was twenty years his senior) the two men
became great friends. In 1887, when Lamoureux gave the first
performance in Paris of *Lohengrin*, van Dyck sang the principal
role with such success that Cosima Wagner invited him to
Munich to give an audition as a result of which he was engaged
on the spot to sing *Parsifal* at Bayreuth the following year. But
first it was necessary for him to learn German, and so van Dyck
decided to go to Karlsruhe to study his new role under Felix
Mottl, who was then in charge of the grand-ducal Opera there.
For the sequence of events which led to Chabrier's first meeting
with Mottl we cannot do better than turn to a letter which van
Dyck wrote in after years to his friend, the French music critic
Robert Brussel, who at the time was planning to write a life of
Chabrier.[2] It is dated 'Bayreuth, 19th July 1911, 21 Blumen-
strasse', and in it van Dyck describes how Chabrier came to see
him off when he left Paris to join Mottl in Karlsruhe on that
day in 1887:

> Chabrier insisted on accompanying me to the station—
> Chabrier, Lamoureux's assistant, was my closest friend and
> my master. From 1883 (the year of my *débuts* at the Lamou-
> reux concerts) until my *Lohengrin* in 1887 I worked practically
> every day with Chabrier—and when I had worked well he
> would play me one of his latest compositions. . . . Just as the
> train was moving Chabrier embraced me, and with an arm round
> my neck, his last words were: 'When you see Mottl, old boy
> (he pronounced it Motte), tell him to do my *Gwendoline*; you're
> a good friend of mine, tell him loud and clear—he'll do it, the
> old rascal!' As soon as I was settled in my little furnished
> flat in the Seminarstrasse I talked to Mottl about *Gwendoline*.
> He was enthusiastic. . . . And as I spoke about Chabrier as a
> composer, and not only as my friend, Mottl immediately

wanted to make his acquaintance—and the next thing was that
Emmanuel arrived in Karlsruhe. Rehearsals of *Gwendoline*
started immediately. You know the rest. But what I can't
describe are the delightful days I spent with Mottl and Chabrier in Karlsruhe . . . Mlle Mailhac as Gwendoline was admirable, and Karlsruhe gave Chabrier a triumphant ovation!

In a letter written twenty-four years after the events described
therein took place a certain amount of chronological foreshorten-
ing is to be expected, and in point of fact it was not until
30th May 1889 that *Gwendoline* was finally produced in Karlsruhe. But correspondence between Chabrier and Mottl began in
the autumn of 1887, and in December of that year Chabrier met
Mottl for the first time in Karlsruhe where they discussed the
details of the promised production of *Gwendoline*. Writing to
Mottl from Paris on 31st January 1888, Chabrier expresses his
pleasure at the turn events had taken and the prospect of seeing
his opera produced in Germany:

Cher ami,

   You can imagine how I was besieged with questions on my
return to Paris! It was Mottl here and Mottl there; we talked
of nothing but of you and of the great works which you conduct like the great artist you are, you wonderful man! I shall
never forget your kindness and hospitality during my stay in
Karlsruhe, and I hope to be able to prove to you when you
come to visit our dear Paris that I am not ungrateful. As I
told you, I have to go to Berlin and Vienna, and would be glad
if you could recommend me warmly to the Kapellmeisters
in these two capitals. We will talk about this in Karlsruhe,
because I shall arrive there on the morning of the 13th. But
I shall not stay for more than two days, after which I and my
publisher will be off to Berlin. I would be grateful, my dear
friend, if you could arrange on the afternoon of the 13th
for Mlle Mailhac and MM. Plank and Oberlander to hear a
run-through of *Gwendoline*; I am very anxious for these artists

to hear the complete work, and I will bring a copy of the score
with a complete German translation. I will sing it for them to
the best of my ability. I'll ask you in advance, my dear Mottl,
to forgive me for the trouble I'm causing you, but I must tell
you in all sincerity that I consider it a great compliment to
have my work performed in Karlsruhe, and an honour to have
you to conduct it.

I should be so delighted if I could hear on the 13th or the
14th either *Walküre* or *Götterdämmerung*—or perhaps *Benvenuto*
—in any case you promised, before I go, to put on something
interesting, and I hope you will keep your word! [3] Write me a
line—it doesn't matter if your French is not too good, or, if
in German, my publisher will translate—but don't leave me
without news of you.

Remember me, please, to Mlle Mailhac, and with the
warmest of handshakes, believe me, my dear friend,

your devoted
Emmanuel Chabrier.

Chabrier's object in visiting Vienna was primarily to see Hans
Richter, and on his way back, via Berlin, he wrote from the
latter capital to Mottl on 21st February 1888 to report on his
meeting with the great man:

Dear friend,

I was delighted with my visit to your native town—a lovely
city and lovely women! Your letter to Richter was most
effective; I had two meetings with him, one concerning
Gwendoline and the other about *Le Roi malgré lui*.

Richter was evidently *very, very* satisfied, but he gave me to
understand that what they wanted here was an opéra-comique
rather than an *opera*, and so I think that *Le Roi* will suit them
best. Jahn and Richter will have in a few days the libretto of
Le Roi, and if they approve will put on the work immediately.[4]
You see we haven't lost any time and, thanks to your excellent recommendations, we have made good use of it.

Here, in Berlin, they don't seem to work so much as in Karlsruhe. Bock, the publisher whom we saw this morning, told us that nothing new had been produced for the last two years, and that I would find it difficult to get my music performed; it wasn't usual for Berlin to *launch* a new work; it rarely took the initiative, but when towns like Karlsruhe, Hamburg, Leipzig or Cologne had successes it would take note of the fact. However, tomorrow I shall see Count Hopsberg, the Intendant, and see what he has to say. After that we are going on to Brunswick, where Enoch has business, and then to Cologne. Could you send me *immediately* a letter of introduction to the Kapellmeister of Cologne? Please address your letter to M. Emmanuel Chabrier, c/o M. Litolff, publisher, Brunswick. I shall be there on Thursday and Friday—I hope to have an audition at Cologne—and I should be back in my old Paris Sunday or Monday at the latest.

From Brunswick Chabrier wrote to his wife to tell her about going to the theatre with Litolff and having supper with him afterwards, with oysters, 'entrecôte à la Béarnaise', grouse, dessert, choice wines and a good Kümmel 'pour pousser la digestion'. Here we get a glimpse of Chabrier, the *bon vivant*, appreciating the good things of the earth, while in the next sentence we see him once again as an artist with a keen eye for beauty, always interested in his surroundings and taking pleasure in describing them just as he did when writing home as a young man on his first trip abroad to Holland and Belgium.

Brunswick is the most German, the most medieval, the most curious town I have ever visited. It is a marvel; all the time I wished you could be with me; you would have been astonished at every step. In summer it must be enchanting, but now there is a good foot of snow everywhere, and this white mantle is rather sad and makes everything misty: *one can't see enough*. It's even more picturesque than Nuremberg, we are told. But maybe the inhabitants of Nuremberg would not agree.

In any case it's delicious—I'll explain all this to you when we
meet. . . . Take care of the little one; embrace our Marcel
for me—and best greetings to Nanine. I am beginning to
need 'la maman' [this is how he always addressed his wife].

Your own
Emmanuel.

It was about this time, while he was waiting impatiently for some
definite news about the fate of his operas in Germany and Vienna,
that he started work on what was to be his last work, the opera
Briséïs for which Catulle Mendès once again, in collaboration with
Ephraïm Mikhaël, had supplied a libretto based on Goethe's
tale, *The Bride of Corinth*. He was able to complete only one act,
and died without ever hearing it performed. He attached the
greatest importance to this work, and used to carry the score
about with him everywhere. It contains some remarkable music
which we shall be examining in a later chapter. It is a tribute to
Chabrier's restless energy and appetite for composition, once he
had decided on this career, that he was continually on the look-
out for new themes and forming projects which, even if they
came to nothing, are evidence of his lively mind and interest in a
great variety of subjects. Thus, for example, even while he was
engaged on the composition of *Le Roi malgré lui* he was already
thinking of writing another opera, hesitating between Shake-
speare's *The Tempest* and Pushkin's *The Captain's Daughter*. In the
event nothing came of either project, but this habit of perpetually
forming plans which eventually had to be abandoned was a trait
which he shared with many other composers, notably Debussy
and Ravel.

It was fortunate that he had this new opera, *Briséïs*, to keep
him occupied; for as the months went by there was still no definite
news from Mottl about the promised production of *Gwendoline*,
and in the summer of 1888 Chabrier had another disappointment.
He had planned to go to Bayreuth to hear his friend van Dyck in
Parsifal, and it had been arranged that while there he should meet

Cosima Wagner. But in August both his wife and his mother-in-law fell ill and it was impossible for him to leave his family. He was also becoming more and more apprehensive about the long delayed production of *Gwendoline* in Karlsruhe, especially as he had heard rumours that Mottl might be leaving to take up another post in Budapest and thus might be unable after all to mount the opera before he went. He therefore continued to bombard both Mottl and van Dyck with letters in which he did not attempt to conceal his impatience. Finally Mottl wrote (in German) to Chabrier's publisher Enoch expressing surprise that they both seemed to assume that *Gwendoline* would not be produced in the course of the present season, and assuring them that the delay had been partly due to the illness of Fritz Planck, the baritone who was to sing the part of Harald, but that nevertheless the opera was due for performance in April next year, provided that Planck would be fit to sing by then. But he would not accept an inferior substitute:

> for I am very keen to do this opera, but I owe it to Chabrier and to the musical world in general to give a performance of this work of the high standard it deserves, and to do that I must have a really brilliant artist for the part of Harald, and I am sure both you and Chabrier would agree with me on this point. . . . The doctor thinks that Planck will be well enough to start rehearsals after Christmas, and I have every hope that the work will make a triumphant entry into Germany in the merry month of April to the satisfaction of us all. . . .

In the event, as Planck's illness continued, a substitute had to be found after all, and it was a baritone named Rathiens who sang the important role of Harald when at last *Gwendoline* made her bow on the stage of the grand-ducal theatre of Karlsruhe on 30th May 1889—a month later than Mottl had predicted.

The *première* was a great success, and Chabrier wrote enthusiastically to his friend van Dyck:

> It's happened at last, my good Ernest! You wanted your old

Chabrier to have his *Gwendoline* played in Karlsruhe: now she
has been—twice—and with what art and devotion on the part
of Mottl, Mailhac [the soprano], the chorus, that admirable
orchestra and everyone concerned—and, I may say, an enthusiastic reception from the *Publicum*. Your old Chabrier was
called before the curtain, and there they were, all applauding
madly, two rows of officers and all the regular Karlsruhe first-
nighters . . . and my Ernest wasn't there [van Dyck was singing
in Bayreuth].

The opera was given several times that summer and again in
September; and at one of these performances Mottl had written
on the back of the poster advertising the opera: 'My dear Chabrier,
Mme Wagner was here last night and was altogether satisfied with
your work which had the same success as before.'

It was this success that prompted the directors of other pro-
vincial operas to put on *Gwendoline*, and the following year, as
already stated, it was performed in Leipzig, Dresden and Munich;
in 1891 in Stuttgart, and in 1893 in Düsseldorf. But despite the
intervention of Mottl and Richter, Chabrier's hopes of seeing
it done in Vienna was never realized. It was in Munich that it
had the greatest success, remaining in the repertory from November 1890 until February 1891 under the direction of Hermann
Levi. While in Munich Chabrier met the painter Franz von
Lenbach (1836–1904) whom he described in a letter to his old
nurse Nanine (with whom he corresponded regularly) as 'Germany's greatest painter, and a very rich man who lives in a
veritable palace'. Nothing throws more light on the fundamental
character of this profoundly sincere, lovable and goodhearted
man than his devotion to his old nurse (whose pet name for him
was 'Mavel')—a devotion so strong that when he heard in
Bayreuth, where he had gone in the summer of 1889, that she
had been stricken with paralysis he did not hesitate to cut his
visit short in order to be at her bedside. As he wrote to Mottl:

Ernest will have told you I was obliged to leave precipitately

1. Chabrier's birthplace—view from the street

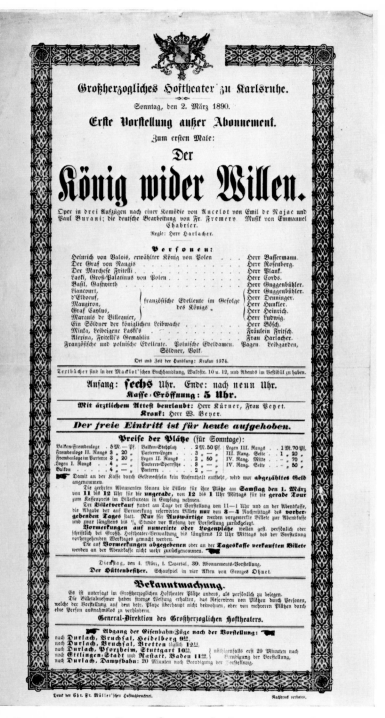

2. Poster announcing first performance in Germany at Karlsruhe of
Le Roi malgré lui

3. Caricature of Chabrier by Detaille

△ 4. *Autour du Piano*
Fantin-Latour. Fr
left to right: (fo
ground) Emmanue
Chabrier, Edmon
Maître, Amédée
Pigeon; (back row)
Adolphe Jullien,
A. Boisseau, Cami
Benoît, Antoine L
caux, Vincent d'In
The score is *Carme*

◁ 5. Chabrier with V
Dyck (1890)

6. Portrait of Chabrier (1881) by Manet

Théâtre National

DE L'OPÉRA

CABINET DU DIRECTEUR

Paris, le 1er mars 1.89

Mon cher Maître

(Chabrier)

Je suis très heureux de vous donner une bonne nouvelle qui j'espère, hâtera votre guérison –

Gwendoline, votre belle œuvre, que Paris devrait avoir entendue depuis longtemps, sera

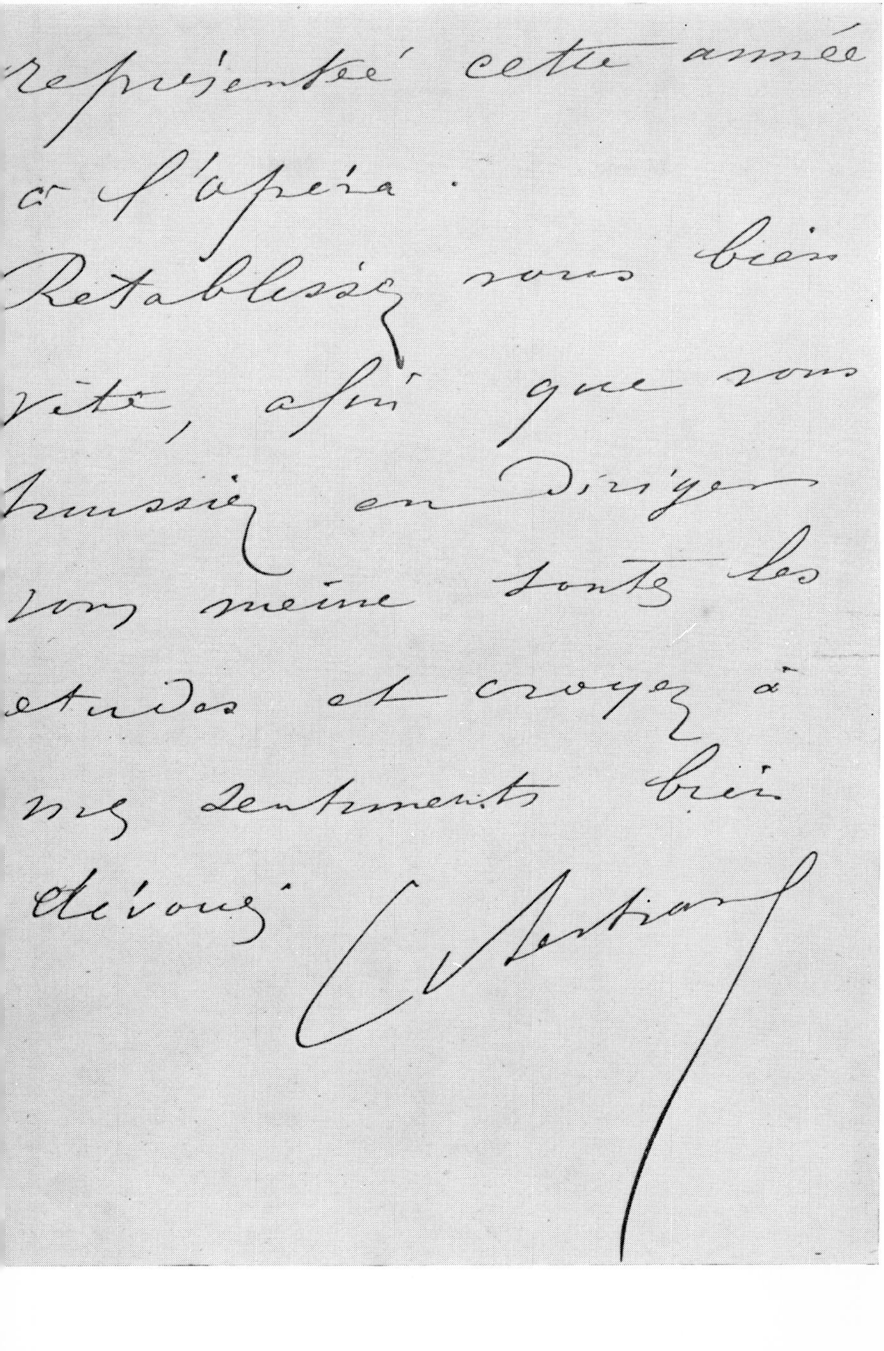

représentée cette année

à l'opéra.

Rétablissez vous bien

vite, afin que vous

puissiez en Diriger

vous même toutes les

etudes et croyez à

mes sentiments bien

dévoués   L Bertrand

7. Letter from the Director of the Paris Opéra (1893) with the news
that *Gwendoline* had been accepted

8. Chabrier at Wimereux (1887)

as my poor old nurse is seriously ill and my being absent has
made her suffer more. She kept saying: 'I shan't see my
Emmanuel now before I die!' But she has seen me, the dear
woman, and she is better—but alas! I fear it will be a long
illness. We can only hope . . .

Nanine, whose real name was Anne Delayre, never recovered
from her stroke and died in a nursing home at Arcueil early in
1891—just three years before her beloved master. She had been
with the Chabriers since the age of eighteen, and had worked
without wages towards the end of her life when the Chabriers'
financial situation had deteriorated. But when she died, she left
her entire savings, amounting to eight thousand francs, to
Chabrier's two sons.

It must have been a great disappointment for Chabrier to leave
Bayreuth so suddenly, thus cutting short the treat to which he
had for so long looked forward; but at least he had the satisfaction
of hearing, before he departed, *Parsifal* (for the first time),
Tristan and the *Meistersinger*. Of *Parsifal* he wrote enthusiastically
to his wife (Tiénot; printed in *Comoedia*, 22nd December 1913):

> . . . Yesterday, Sunday, 21st July 1889, I heard *Parsifal* for
> the first time. I have never in all my life had an artistic experi-
> ence at all comparable to this; it is overwhelming; one comes
> out after each act (I do, at least) absolutely overcome with
> admiration, bewildered, distraught with tears running down
> one's cheeks. It's worse than *Tristan* in 1880. What can I say?
> I have never heard anything like it. It is sublime from begin-
> ning to end. . . . And what a performance! Van Dyck quite
> extraordinary; he's a very great artist. And the chorus! And
> the orchestra! In a word, it was perfection, ideal, beyond
> everything. It's useless to look for anything more; it's un-
> believable to have found this!

Although this language sounds almost hysterical to our ears today,
it must be remembered that Chabrier was not alone among

French musicians to be affected in this way, especially by
Parsifal; even Debussy (who, by the way, was paying his second
and last visit to Bayreuth in 1889 and must have been there at
the same time as Chabrier), despite his later rejection of Wagner's
aesthetic, was haunted all his life by *Parsifal* ('one of the most
beautiful monuments ever raised to music'), being especially
impressed by what he called its 'orchestral infallibility'—
a quality he also discerned in the score of *Petruchka*. And of
course there are moments in his own *Le Martyre de Saint
Sébastien* and even in *Pelléas* where the spectre of *Parsifal* looms
unmistakably.

The French contingent of pilgrims to Bayreuth that year was a
strong one and included, besides Chabrier, Chausson, Vincent
d'Indy, de Bréville, Lamoureux, Chevillard, Robert Godet
(Debussy's great friend with whom he corresponded regularly)
and the painter Jacques-Emile Blanche. Chabrier was invited by
Cosima Wagner to supper at Wahnfried, where he played *España*
and the Overture to *Gwendoline* to her on the piano, and afterwards took home with him as a souvenir a sprig of ivy from
Wagner's tomb in the garden. (This was one of the exhibits at the
Chabrier centenary exhibition at the Paris Opéra-Comique in
1941.) He was also shown all over the famous theatre, but was
somewhat critical of Wagner's idea of having the orchestra under
the stage:

> I am not sure that I altogether approve of this [he wrote to
> his wife], a lot of detail is lost in this way; the music seems to
> come from a distance, as if from a room next door. It's all
> right in the *fortes*, but in quieter and polyphonic passages I
> lose half the sound . . .

Chabrier was by now beginning to be well known in Germany,
and for this he was deeply indebted to Felix Mottl with whom
now he had become on very friendly terms; the two men were
now 'tutoying' one another, and Chabrier was sometimes almost
too fulsome in his admiration for everything that Mottl did, and

at the same time very conscious of what he owed to him. After
his premature departure from Bayreuth he wrote:

> Let me once more thank you for all your kindnesses to me
> over there; what a joy it was for me to hear you at the head
> of that orchestra when you conducted so superbly that
> admirable *Tristan* . . . well, carry on with your triumphs, and
> remember that I shall never forget what you have done for
> me. Do not forget your cordially devoted
>
> Emmanuel Chabrier.

As it turned out, Mottl was to do still more for him, for as a
result of the success of *Gwendoline*, he had now decided to produce
Le Roi malgré lui. This meant that for the next year or so affairs in
Germany would again claim a great deal of Chabrier's time.

CHAPTER SEVEN

1888–1891—Le Roi malgré lui *in Germany*—At home, *Prélude pastoral, Joyeuse Marche, Six mélodies*—Life in Touraine—*Failing health, family and financial worries.*

ALTHOUGH THE composition and production of *Gwendoline* and *Le Roi* and the success of the former in Germany had been for Chabrier the most important events in his career so far, he nevertheless found time during these years to compose a number of other smaller scale works, some of which are among those by which he is perhaps best known today. And so, before returning to Germany to relate events connected with the production there of *Le Roi malgré lui*, it is time now to see what in the meantime he had been doing in other fields. So far as the general public is concerned, the name of Chabrier is associated, mainly if not exclusively, with two of his most extrovert and 'popular' works—*España* and *Joyeuse Marche*. The latter was composed in 1888 and conducted by the composer at a festival of his music at Angers in November of the same year. Contrary to what is generally believed, the work was originally written for the piano, although in most catalogues this version is usually described as a transcription. Alfred Cortot, however, is categoric on this point, and calls attention to the fact that all the most striking orchestral effects are already present in the piano version—which is not surprising since Chabrier invariably composed at the piano, and much of his keyboard writing has, in any case, a definite orchestral flavour which is very characteristic of the composer, and also of his style of playing, to judge from contemporary accounts of those who heard him give one of his astonishing virtuoso displays.[1] Cortot (1948) has found exactly the right words in which to describe the irresistible impact of this music:

. . . the truculent flavour, unbuttoned and cheeky exuberance of this Carnavalesque fantasia . . . with its incomparable rhythmic sensuality and amusing contrapuntal jokes. This kind of *bouffonnerie* belongs to Chabrier alone. Neither in Hervé nor in Offenbach could one find this kind of drollery that derives from the music itself, the rhythmic dislocation and a kind of harmonic humour which cracks a joke with a well-placed six-four chord. . . . In claiming for *Joyeuse Marche* the place to which it is entitled in Chabrier's pianistic output, we are not doing so for the sake of exactitude and correct classification, but rather so that the repertory of interpreters of the master of musical humour may be enriched by a work of a burlesque character which it had not hitherto included.

When Chabrier conducted its first performance at Angers it was billed as *Marche française*. Later it became *Marche joyeuse* and was played as such at its first performance in Paris at a Société Nationale concert in 1889; and it was not until Lamoureux conducted it the following year that it assumed the title by which it is universally known today.

Julien Tiérsot after the Société Nationale concert wrote in *Le Ménéstrel*:

M. Chabrier's piece was the high-spot of the evening; impossible to have more verve, more gaiety and life; with its unexpected sonorities the exaggeration of which produces comical effects, the piece was enthusiastically encored. Those who were present at this concert will not be able to say any more that the Société Nationale is boring . . .

The work is dedicated to Vincent d'Indy and scored for a large orchestra including four bassoons, four horns, two cornets in C, two trumpets in F; three trombones and tuba, kettledrums, side drum, triangle, cymbals, two harps and usual strings. Marked ' *Tempo di marcia, molto risoluto e giocoso* ', it is expertly orchestrated, most effective in performance and does not go on too long; Chabrier, like a good *raconteur*, always knows when to stop.

Another of his works performed on this occasion at Angers was the somewhat mysterious *Prélude pastoral*, which for some reason was never published and after its second performance in Paris in 1889 had to wait until 1943 before being heard again, apparently for the last time. On that occasion it was conducted by the late Claude Delvincourt (one time Director of the Paris Conservatoire) with the orchestra of the Société des Concerts du Conservatoire, 12th December 1943). This work, which Chabrier also referred to as the *Andante in F*, is not to be confused with the *Suite pastorale* (performed at the same concert) which denotes the orchestral version (made by the composer) of four of the *Dix pièces pittoresques* for piano: *Idylle*, *Danse villageoise*, *Sous-bois* and *Scherzo-Valse*. To judge from the notices it received in the local press after the Angers performance the *Prélude* made a considerable impression. Thus, a critic in the revue *Angers-Artiste* described it as

> a superb instrumental piece, built on a remarkably well designed theme with some ingenious counterpoint. It contains some orchestral effects the breadth and amplitude of which reveal the influence of Richard Wagner.

Another local critic also referred to the *Prélude*'s Wagnerian sonorities, but found that this in no way diminished his admiration of the 'puissance si personnelle du maître français', adding that the work called for a first-class orchestra to cope with such complicated music.[2]

Another work that figured in the programme of the Chabrier festival at Angers in 1888 was the orchestral version of the *Habanera*, originally written for the piano and published in 1885. This is an unimportant and not very distinguished composition reproducing all the effects of the conventional Habanera-Tango, drawing-room model.

On the other hand, the *Six mélodies*, published in 1890, are pure Chabrier and could have been written by no one else. He was now spending a good deal of his time in the country at La Membrolle, and was surrounded by the sights and sounds of country life. It was then that he had the idea of setting to music some amusing little thumb-nail sketches in verse written by Edmond Rostand and Rosemonde Gérard of such familiar farmyard characters as pigs and ducks and turkeys, and even the shrill cicadas whose loud chirping in the noonday heat is so evocative of the French countryside in summer. What Chabrier called his 'little barnyard suite' consisted then of the following: *Villanelle des petits canards*; *Ballade des gros dindons*; *Pastorale des cochons roses*; and *Les Cigales*. The other two songs in this collection were *L'Île heureuse* and *Toutes les fleurs* cast in a far more conventional mould and coming more into the category of the drawing-room ballad. (He himself, in a letter to van Dyck, to whom the latter song is dedicated, spoke of it as being 'd'un baveux de salon irrésistible'—literally 'drawing-room gush'—but Poulenc thinks the term did not have for him the pejorative sense it has for us because Chabrier 'believed' in his tunes as all true musicians do today.)

In the farmyard songs, however, Chabrier in a sense made musical history with these comical sketches in which the salient features of each of the creatures portrayed are underlined with a most disarming mixture of irony, humour and realism, from which even romance (as in the *Pastorale des cochons roses*) is not altogether absent. There are not many instances in music of humorous animal portraits, and these pieces have nothing in common with the stylized sophistication of Rameau's *Poule* or Daquin's *Coucou*, or even with Beethoven's ornithological nature notes in the *Pastoral* which are there simply as 'background' effects which are part of the landscape. For Chabrier looks at his ducks and pigs and turkeys with a humorous twinkle in his eye, and sees them as individuals—the waddling ducks like rather simple country bumpkins, the naïve little rosy pigs with their corkscrew tails and beady eyes reminding one of a *galantin*, and the pompous turkeys resembling nothing so much as a bevy of

self-important aldermen or rather shady business men in con-
ference. The music for the little pigs is in a mock-romantic vein
with some beautifully turned cadences and intriguing harmonies;
the ducks have a simple, square-cut little marching tune; the
ponderous gait of the turkeys is rendered by a comically emphatic
little figure, strongly accented, and each couplet (for some reason
known only to Chabrier), is rounded off by a quotation from the
Serenade from *Don Giovanni*. . . .

What is especially interesting about these little songs is that
they introduced a new note into contemporary French music and
were clearly the forerunners of Ravel's *Histoires naturelles*, which
did not appear until 1909. It is true that Saint-Saëns had actually
composed his *Carnaval des animaux* in 1886 (four years before
Chabrier's *Petits cochons roses*), but no one outside a small circle
of intimate friends knew of their existence during the composer's
lifetime as they were not published until after his death in 1921.
It is, of course, conceivable that Chabrier may have known about
them, but there is no evidence at all that he did; and in any case
he was the first 'serious' composer to publish such frivolities
without hesitation or false shame. In a letter to a friend he admits
that he was paid well for them, but adds: 'They are artistic
enough to be worth taking pains over, and this I have done.'
Ravel's approach to Jules Renard's dry little pen-pictures of a
peacock, a swan, a guineafowl, a kingfisher and a cricket was
considerably more sophisticated in every way than Chabrier's
had been; but in his harmonic formula for the cricket (*Le Grillon*)
winding up her little watch he has made what amounts to an
actual crib of Chabrier's ingenious way of suggesting the shrill
chirping of the cicadas in his *Les Cigales*.

The farmyard pieces (what Chabrier called his 'petites bougreries'
—little bits of nonsense) appeared in 1890, and were written
while he was engaged on the opera on which he had been working
for the last two years but of which he was only to complete one
act before he died—his beloved *Briséis*—and while he was waiting
for the final arrangements to be made for the production of *Le*

Roi malgré lui in Karlsruhe. Felix Mottl wrote to him from Vienna
on 16th September 1889:

> My dear Chabrier,
>
> We have just finished (Flesch and I) our fourth reading of
> *Le Roi malgré lui*. We are absolutely enchanted with your
> masterpiece, and we drink to the health of the *maître* Chabrier!
> Vivat, crescat, floreat!
>
> > Felix Mottl, Friedrich Flesch,
> >
> > > Fritz (he's my nephew who is
> > > also enchanted!)
>
> Would you be good enough to send to Flesch (Unter St
> Veit, nr Vienna) a few photographs of your physiognomy
> (so handsome?) for display in the music shops in Vienna.
> We have sworn that you will be the most popular man in
> Vienna in the next fortnight![3]

It was not, however, until late in October that the full score
and parts of *Le Roi* finally reached Mottl in Karlsruhe, and owing
to various unforeseen delays and hindrances it was not until
March of the next year that the opera was eventually produced,
one of the reasons for the delay being the death in January 1890
of the Empress Augusta, which meant that the Court in the
Grand Duchy of Baden had to go into mourning. Meanwhile
Mottl wrote to Cosima Wagner to tell her that rehearsals on *Le
Roi* had started, but added that he did not think it would please
her at all—much less than *Gwendoline*—as parts of it were rather
common ('er hat mitunter etwas sehr ordinäres'), although it was
impossible not to recognize a great talent ('eine starke Begabung').

Chabrier went over to Karlsruhe again for the *première* for
which he had waited so impatiently and was given a great reception.
Arriving a few days before the great event, he wrote to his wife to
tell her he had been invited to a smart evening party where he met

> all the local high-life; all the women in black or white
> because of mourning for Augusta, and the men in frock-

coats. I was given an ovation; I played, and also accompanied Fritsch [Frl. Fritsch, who took the part of Minka] in the Gipsy Song (in Act II) which she does very well. Then Mottl sat down at the piano and at the first bars of the *Blue Danube* your old man started waltzing like a jack-in-the-box. I was much fêted; all the cream of Karlsruhe society was there and will be at the opera again on Sunday—that's why poor old Mottl dragged me there, to exhibit me and get me to meet people; he's marvellous, that man, he really is. . . . The Duke of Baden asked to see me; he wants to give me some decoration and got Mottl to sound me out as to whether I should like that —for political reasons, you understand. I replied that being in Karlsruhe I was under orders from the Grand Duke and that seeing that I had come here to ask the good people of Baden to play my works it would be caddish indeed for me to despise or stupidly refuse the mark of distinction their Grand Duke was anxious to confer upon me. He even told Mottl to treat with special consideration any artists who came to Karlsruhe. Here I'm only an artist; they've taken a liking for me and they show it, and I'm everywhere very well received; and, as a Frenchman, I'm very flattered. I don't throw myself at them, but wait for them to come to me; but when they do— and they all do—I obviously can't run away! There is a time for everything. My patriotism is by no means weakened by these contacts; on the contrary, it is strengthened, and I have my own ways of proving it by showing them a Frenchman who is not a nobody. . . . If my Government didn't spend 800,000 frs. a year for the Opéra to produce *Lucie*, [4] there would be no need for me to be using my shoe-leather in the Kaiserstrasse; but when I find it difficult or impossible to sell my own works at home I export them—and that's all there is to it. . . . At the party I told you about I had to turn out at least a dozen autographs for a bevy of fine ladies!— there was no end to it! . . . Your old

Emmanuel.

This letter is interesting psychologically for the light it throws on three facets of Chabrier's character: the sense of grievance he carried all his life at being, as he imagined rightly or wrongly, underestimated in his own country; his fundamental honesty; and a certain rather naïve delight in being flattered and treated as an important person together with an enormous capacity for enjoying himself in all sorts of situations. The first night was a great success, and the next day Chabrier wrote again to his wife to tell her all about it:

. . . The theatre was *packed*. Everything went marvellously, and I had to appear on stage after each act. Throughout the whole performance I was on stage in my tails and white tie supervising the movements, beating time, often just mechanically because no one was looking at me—but no matter, I was in the middle of things. It was a terrific success. Fritsch is extraordinary, Plank [as Fritelli] most amusing and the perfect tenor. . . . Last night, after the show, a big supper party with all the artists; tomorrow at 10 rehearsal in the theatre; luncheon at 1 with the Grand Duke, and supper in the evening chez Fritsch. Wednesday, second performance of *Le Roi* in Baden, and home on Thursday. Thursday night dinner with my little wife . . . I got André's little letter. . . . I can hardly keep awake. . . . Your old

Emmanuel.

Meanwhile Mottl had written to Cosima Wagner to report on the opera's reception as follows:

Karlsruhe, 6th March 1890.
. . . Chabrier was there and had us all turned upside-down by his vivaciousness, and gay but not superficial character! The opera undoubtedly gains a lot in performance in the theatre, and on the second night it went very well and I was, on the whole, very pleased with it. Chabrier has been fêted on a really grandiose and spectacular scale, which has made him

very happy. The Grand Duke told him he looked upon him as
a messenger of peace since he came to bring harmony; and he
made him some other equally gracious compliments. One
thing is certain: this man is enormously talented, and by
comparison with our own wretched German note-spinners a
man like him seems really great.

It will be remembered that Mottl had warned Cosima that *Le
Roi* would probably not be to her taste—and he was right. It
must, however, have been something of a shock for him when he
received from her the following letter, written after she had seen
the opera in Dresden a month later:

On Saturday I saw *Le Roi malgré lui* in Dresden. It is nothing
more or less than rubbish from A to Z! Neither God nor
Mottl could make it any better. Heavens above, what vulgarity, and what poverty of ideas! Offenbach, Meyerbeer
and Gounod, with some tricks of orchestration *à la* Berlioz.
Why Chabrier should have come to Bayreuth will no doubt
always remain a mystery. As I was leaving the theatre with
Countess Wolkenstein we agreed that there was at least one
good thing, and that was that never again would one have to
listen to a single note by Chabrier. If *Gwendoline* was bad,
this is abominable. He can't even write a passable dance. In
the first act I was horrified, in the second I was furious, in the
third so overcome [*niedergeschlagen*] that I was asking myself once more what on earth I was doing in that *galère*. The
performance was good. Scheidemann played the King, and the
orchestra under Schuch was very lively and played with spirit.
But no performance in the world could ever, even for an instant, disguise these café-concert trivialities, the lowest of the
low, which leave one with a really bestial impression.
['. . . diese niedrigste Café-chantant-Trivialität . . . sie dringt
zu einem in bestialischer Weise.'] On my return I got someone to play to me all the evening the mazurkas of Chopin to
convince me that, even apart from the greatest geniuses, there

is still some delicacy, some sensibility, some imagination and some graciousness left in the world. How is it that all these clowns make music? ['Wie kommen nur alle diese Grobiane zur Musik?'] Ah, if it were only vulgarity. . . . But there is something else, a whole world that makes you shudder. . . . It's not a bad thing that the minstrel [Spielmann] should make an error of taste for once. In spite of everything he's still Felix—and minstrel and king as well. But I must relieve my feelings of anger, which otherwise would be gnawing at my heart.

The violence of this reaction seems out of all proportion to the occasion which provoked it, and reveals a narrowness of outlook and a disagreeable priggishness which confound the imagination, even when due allowance is made for the conventional Teutonic mentality of one conditioned only to belief in the 'sublime'. It shows too a curious lack of critical discrimination which, had she possessed it, would have enabled a woman of Cosima Wagner's intelligence to discern, even in music of a genre with which she personally had little sympathy, evidence of superior craftsman-ship and genuine musical accomplishment of a very high order. At any rate the incident underlines the fact that, in spite of his alleged Wagnerian affinities, it was the essential Frenchness of Chabrier's music that always made the strongest impression on all who heard it. It may well have been the knowledge that Chabrier was one of the first musicians in France to recognize and publicly acclaim the greatness and importance of Wagner that endeared him to the Germans—for a time, at any rate—and made it possible for him to have his operas produced in Germany more easily than in his own country. But what really appealed to them in his music was its Gallicism and not its indebtedness, real or imaginary, to any Germanic model. This, incidentally, explains why Felix Mottl, as a Viennese, admired and understood it so readily and spontaneously and was prepared to introduce it to German audiences in those areas in which he was free to enlarge the current repertory in any way he pleased. Even at the risk, as we have seen, of displeasing Frau Cosima. . . .

Before leaving Karlsruhe Chabrier wrote once more to his wife describing his visit to the Grand Duke—'the local Carnot' as he called him—who told him that he was delighted that a French composer should be applauded in Karlsruhe, adding that their two countries were destined to be friends, and that he was profoundly touched by the presence of 'an *eminent* artist'. Chabrier comments:

> It was he who thanked me!!! He received me in full dress, with some terrific hand-shaking. Of course he's a German, but seems a very good fellow [*il a l'air bon comme le pain*]. Then we went to lunch with his brother, Prince William, who's even more handsome. He came to the door to receive us; all these people speak French astonishingly well. . . . At table I knew nearly everyone since for the last week I've been rubbing shoulders with all the local celebrities. There were fifteen of us; after lunch, which was exquisite, we had coffee, liqueurs and cigarettes; the waltz from *Le Roi* on an Erard and piano duets with Mottl. We didn't break up till half past three. You've no idea how polite these people are. My host said he was *honoured* to have me as his guest!!!

In the autumn of that year Chabrier went to Munich for the *première* of *Gwendoline*, which Hermann Levi conducted, and went straight back to Paris without passing again through Carlsruhe.

In February 1891 he wrote to Mottl, with whom by this time he was on intimately friendly terms—'mon petit cher Momottl . . . mon très cher Felix . . . mon petit coco', etc.—to unburden himself of various private worries which were troubling him at that time and were no doubt partly connected with his gradually failing health. To begin with, he was not satisfied with the way he felt his two boys were neglecting their studies and failing to make any progress:

> I get into mad rages with them; I can't make them study or

work properly; it's no good people telling me that'll come *later*; it's *now* that I want to see them getting down to things seriously, so I have to be their schoolmaster, and that takes up a lot of my time and makes me hopping mad.

Chabrier was also worried because he felt his financial position was insecure and for some time his wife had been a semi-invalid unable to do very much in the house. And now, to make matters worse, his beloved old Nanine had died. In telling Mottl about this he reminded him how he had to leave Bayreuth two years ago when Nanine had had her stroke.

All this has made me very depressed. There are periods like this in life, times that are hard to bear, and unfortunately for me, I'm one of those people, in spite of my jovial appearance, who feel very deeply especially about things of this kind.

(Here we have the key to Chabrier's true character; underneath the bluff, hearty, extrovert outer man lay a very sensitive, emotional human being capable of great devotion and affection and entirely without false pretensions.) He was also worried at having made no progress with his new opera *Briséis* for the last four or five months and, to crown it all, his hopes of seeing *Gwendoline* at last produced in Paris were once more dashed to the ground when Henri Verdhurt, who had promised to do it at the Eden Theatre in Paris, once again went bankrupt just as he had in Brussels five years previously when the run of *Gwendoline* was interrupted for the same reason. From now on his correspondence with Mottl, who in the meantime had got married, became less frequent, although the Chabriers were still trying persuade him to visit them in Paris—a visit which in the end only came about when it was too late; Chabrier was by then a dying man.

For the three last years of his life were darkened by the gradu-ally increasing ravages of the general paralysis (probably of syphilitic origin) which impaired his faculties and turned this man, who had been all his life so active, so ebullient and so hard-working, into a hypochondriac continually complaining of his symptoms, of the treatment prescribed for him by his doctors, of his financial worries and above all of his failing powers and inability to finish the score he cherished above all others, that of *Briséis*. In a pathetic letter to his son Marcel, quoted by Poulenc (1961), he writes:

> Your father is not well; the treatment I'm having stupefies me instead of calming and refreshing me. I need some more invigorating medicine—I'll see about this when I come to Paris next month. My head is very tired. . . . Work well, my poor dear boy, and think of your father who wants to go on working near you and to have you at his side. If you have a moment free on Sunday morning, go and say a little prayer for your father on our Nanine's grave; she'll hear that, coming from you, because she loved you very much. . . .

And yet, in the middle of all these difficulties and mental and physical suffering, Chabrier found time and strength to take an active part in organizing a petition to the Minister of Fine Arts in favour of Adolphe Sax (1814–94), who, at the age of seventy-eight, had been proclaimed bankrupt and as a consequence deprived of his Légion d'Honneur. With the backing of Vincent d'Indy, Fauré, Massenet, Saint-Saëns, Reyer and other distinguished musicians, who also signed, Chabrier himself drafted the letter to the Minister in the following terms (Poulenc):

Monsieur le Ministre,

> We the undersigned wish to draw your attention urgently to the distressing situation of Adolphe Sax and to request your intervention in his favour.
> For sixty years Sax has worked in France and for France, his country of adoption.
> One can anticipate the judgment of posterity of describing as the work of a genius the full range of his inventions.
> Sax has revolutionized the manufacture of wind instruments

and brought about an unprecedented advance in this branch of the art.

All his work is based strictly on the discovery of a law of acoustics hitherto unknown or ill-defined, which it has been his triumph to formulate in precise terms.

Sax has discovered and proved that the characteristic timbre of each instrument is produced, not by the nature of the substance of which it is composed—brass, wood or glass—but by the proportions and form of the column of air enclosed in this sonorous substance.

It is this principle, this original idea, that has made possible the numerous families of new instruments which bear his name: Sax-trumpet, Sax-horn, Sax-tuba, Saxophone, etc.

This invention, admirable alike in its conception and its realization, has also resulted in instruments with valves and independent crooks; and this alone would be enough to ensure the fame of its author, who has spent his last penny on perfecting his invention which, as soon as it falls into the public domain, will inevitably replace all the old systems hitherto in use.

Instrument-making, thanks to the inventions of Sax, has risen from almost nothing to become an important and flourishing branch of French industry.

The man who for the last sixty years has continued to make discoveries which have provided a means of livelihood for thousands of workmen and artists, after a lifetime of hard work and unprecedented struggles, has been reduced to poverty, that melancholy consecration of genius. At the age of eighty he is forced to depend on his friends for the necessities of life.

It is in the presence of this misfortune, whose severity is only equalled by its injustice, that we are appealing to you, *Monsieur le Ministre*, to consider the plight of the unfortunate Adolphe Sax and do what is necessary to ensure that in the last days of his life he may be free from want.

Emmanuel Chabrier.

It is a remarkable tribute to the generous spirit of Chabrier and his concern for the sufferings of a fellow artist that he should have made this effort at a time when, according to his friend Pierre de Bréville, Chabrier confided in him that he probably would not see him again for a very long time. 'I am a sick man and, like an animal, I hide myself . . .'

Nevertheless, it appears that although he found composition more and more difficult, he was still able to play the piano, and even spoke, in a letter to Paul Vidal as late as the summer of 1893, of being ready to replace him on some occasion at the Opéra where, he wrote, 'I wouldn't mind showing them that I've still got *mes jolis doigts d'autrefois* . . . it's amazing what progress I've made in the last fortnight. . . . Come early, and I'll give you a nice *apéritif* and play you the first act of *Parsifal* . . .' [5]

The last years of his life, however, were spent largely in the country at La Membrolle, and one of the last occasions on which Chabrier made a public appearance in Paris was at the funeral in 1890 of César Franck when, at the request of Vincent d'Indy, he pronounced the funeral oration. Some embarrassment had been caused by the reluctance of the 'Establishment' (i.e. the Institute and Conservatoire) to associate themselves officially with these public tributes to Franck, who was still, in their eyes, a rebel in the rival camp of the too unorthodox *Schola Cantorum*. Chabrier, who greatly admired Franck though in no sense a follower in his footsteps, rose nobly to the occasion; and d'Indy, in his biography of César Franck, has preserved for us the text of his moving and eloquent peroration:

> *Adieu, Maître, et merci*, for you have done well! We salute in you one of the greatest artists of our century as well as the incomparable teacher whose example has brought into being a whole generation of sturdy, dedicated and serious-minded musicians thoroughly equipped to take part in battles often hard and long-disputed. We salute too in you the just and honest man, so human and devoid of self-interest, who never gave advice that was not sound or uttered a word that was not good. *Adieu!*

CHAPTER EIGHT

Last works—Gwendoline at the Opéra sets seal on his career but comes too late—Death of Chabrier and tributes from French and foreign admirers.

THE LAST three years of his life, though clouded, as we have seen, by sickness and unhappiness, nevertheless saw the creation of three of his major works: *Ode à la musique*; *Bourrée fantasque* and *Briséis*.

Ode à la musique was composed in the winter of 1890 as a kind of 'Consecration of the house' for a musical friend, a certain Jules Griset, to whom it is dedicated; and this explains the inscription on the score 'pour inaugurer la maison d'un ami'. The words, by Edmond Rostand, who was also a friend of Griset, are in praise of music—'Musique adorable. O Déesse!'—and Chabrier has scored the Ode for soprano solo, female chorus and orchestra. The music is in his tenderest, most lyrical vein, and is marked '*Andantino molto con affetto*', and deserves to be better known in this country. Entirely free from any suggestion of eccentricity or pseudo-Wagnerian grandiloquence, it comes from the heart and epitomizes Chabrier's complete and absolute devotion to his art of which, it will be remembered, he once said: 'Never has an artist adored and sought to honour music more than I have; and no one has suffered more in doing so—and so shall I suffer to all eternity.' Again, at the end of his life, when he was struggling against illness and trying to finish his opera despite his failing faculties, we hear a pathetic echo of the same almost lover-like devotion in a letter to his publisher Enoch (Tiénot):

Pauvre chère musique, pauvre chère amie; tu ne veux donc plus que je sois heureux! Je t'aime pourtant, et je crois bien que j'en crèverai. (My poor dear music, my poor dear friend—

so you don't want me to be happy any more! And yet I love
you so much I think this will be the end of me.)

The warmth and spontaneity of this music, with its wealth of
melodic and harmonic invention, make an instant appeal; and
there are some bold touches in the writing for the four-part
chorus and solo voice, as when, for example, while the altos, over
a pedal F sharp in the orchestra, reiterate for four long 9/8 bars
the words 'musique adorable' on the same note, the soloist and
other voices weave round them an expressive melodic figure
starting on a sustained G natural. It is a short work, but beautifully laid out and should be most effective in performance. It
was a great favourite of Debussy's, and was one of the pieces
chosen by Inghelbrecht for the programme he conducted to
inaugurate the brand new Théâtre des Champs-Elysées in April
1913 (just a month before the memorable first performance of
The Rite of Spring). During the rehearsal Debussy was present, and
after the *Ode* had been played Debussy said a few words to the
conductor, who then played it through again. Turning to Debussy,
he asked him if it was better this time, whereupon Debussy
with a smile assured him that it was quite all right the first
time—'but I love this music so much that I wanted to hear it
again'.

The *Ode* had its first performance at a private reception in the
house of the friend for whom it was written in November 1890,
given on this occasion in its original form with piano accompaniment. It was orchestrated soon after and performed for the first
time in public at a Colonne concert in the spring of 1893, since
when it has remained more or less in the repertory in France.
Martineau (1910) mentions a memorable performance in
January 1908 when Mme Jane Bathori was the soloist, Reynaldo
Hahn the conductor and the chorus was composed of Mme
Bathori's pupils. The *Ode à la musique* occupies a very special
place in Chabrier's *œuvre* if only because it is purely and simply
on its merits as a piece of 'straight' music that it must stand or

fall, its limpid and mellifluous accents being completely innocent
of any of those undercurrents of irony, *bravura* or humorous
exaggeration which have come to be accepted as the hallmarks of
his very idiosyncratic style. The *Ode* must be looked upon rather
as the expression of the composer's adoration of his Muse, an
act of homage, simple and sincere.

Very different in style, mood and intention is Chabrier's other
major work belonging to this period, the famous *Bourrée fantasque*
for piano composed, surprisingly enough, in 1891 when his state
of health was causing him and everyone round him grave anxiety.
It is one of the most exciting and original works in the whole
literature of French piano music—and also one of the most
exacting. When Chabrier presented it to the pianist Edouard
Risler to whom it is dedicated, he wrote: 'I'm sending you a
piece in which every note presents a difficulty'—an opinion with
which any amateur confronted with it even today is likely to
agree. It marks a complete breakaway from the conventional
nineteenth-century style of writing for the pianoforte, the instrument here being treated almost like an orchestra, both as regards
timbre and tone-colour. It reveals what Poulenc has called
Chabrier's 'prodigious knowledge of the piano' and embodies
innovations in pianistic technique which foreshadow those
introduced by Ravel in *Gaspard de la nuit* or Debussy in the late
Etudes.

The main theme is hammered out in the middle register of the
piano:

Très animé et avec beaucoup d'entrain (♩ = 152)

developed and put through its paces; and then in the middle
section the mood changes and a sinuous caressing melody is
introduced ('*Istesso tempo; molto espressivo*'), modulating freely and

embroidered with some ingenious and unexpected harmonic progressions, of which the following is an example:

Soon the main theme reappears *pp* in the bass and thereafter is worked in combination with the secondary theme. Eventually it rampages from top to bottom of the keyboard subjected to increasing elaboration and *bravura* treatment, and the piece ends in a blaze of C major exultation. Towards the end, during a momentary lull, there is a curious reminiscence of the undulating bass figure in one of the *Pièces pittoresques* (*Sous-bois*). (*See* Chapter Three, page 34.)

Alfred Cortot, commenting (1948) on the *Bourrée fantasque*, remarks that, until then,

no one had written like this for the piano, investing it with the most unexpected orchestral effects by the use of timbres in conjunction with rhythms and exploiting the impressionist resources of the pedal. This short piano *divertissement* will have done as much, if not more, than *España* to suggest to composers new techniques of musical colour, and its revelations have crossed our frontiers. Albeniz and Granados, in their sumptuous national evocations, have felt its influence, and neither Rimsky-Korsakov, despite his own powers of invention, in *Le Coq d'Or*, nor Stravinsky in *Petruchka*, has been able to forget it.

Chabrier had also told d'Indy about his new composition, and in a letter dated 28th November 1891 (Pincherle, 1946) d'Indy wrote to say how much he was looking forward to playing it:

Cher camarade,

Of course I want to play your 'machine fantasque'! I only hope it won't be too difficult, because now I can't manage runs any more; my fingers are not as agile as they were when I was twenty. But you can be sure I will work hard at it. Impossible to see you today. If you come to the Café Weber tomorrow (I shall be there from 4 p.m.) couldn't we find our way to a piano in the neighbourhood somewhere round six o'clock; then we could go over it together; that would be the best solution. Till tomorrow, in any case; looking forward to shaking your paw.

Vincent d'Indy.

The *Bourrée* was later orchestrated by Felix Mottl and is perhaps as well known in this version as in the original, though the scoring is somewhat heavy-handed and does not always do justice to the original. Charles Koechlin also arranged it for orchestra, but his version was never published. There is also in existence an incomplete arrangement for orchestra made by Chabrier himself which was discovered by the late Roland-Manuel in 1925 among a pile of manuscripts in the possession of the Bretton-Chabrier family. (Commandant Bretton had married the widow of Chabrier's youngest son André, and in honour of his wife's father-in-law had added the name of Chabrier to his own.) Roland-Manuel described his find to the Société française de musicologie in 1938 in a report (published in the same year) containing the following particulars. The MS. consists of sixteen pages of score (about one-third of the whole work) in pencil, as was Chabrier's custom, but with all the tempi and other indications for performance clearly and precisely marked (another invariable habit of Chabrier's, who attached great importance to such details in the execution of his works). It is scored for a small orchestra consisting of piccolo, flute, oboe, two clarinets, bassoon, two horns, two 'pistons' in C, kettle-drums, drum and triangle, usual strings and piano *ad lib*. Both Roland-Manuel and Francis Poulenc have remarked on certain felicitous touches in this orchestration, notably the delicious effect obtained (at the beginning of the *l'istesso tempo* section) by two held notes, an F sharp in the low register of the flute with a B flat in the high register of the bassoon. It is stated in the report that the author had asked Ravel, another of Chabrier's great admirers, if he would care to complete the orchestration, but Ravel declined on the grounds that the sketch was too 'pale' to serve as a basis for a new transcription. Messager, who had also been approached with the same request, was interested, but died (in 1929) before he could examine the score. Another musician who had an opportunity of examining the MS., Ernest Ansermet, told Roland-Manuel that in his opinion Chabrier had a classical feeling for the orchestra, while he had been struck by certain features which he said might well have been signed by Igor Stravinsky.

Edouard Risler, to whom the *Bourrée* is dedicated, did not in fact play it in Chabrier's lifetime, as at the time of its publication he had retired temporarily from the concert platform. However, in a letter to the composer written from Berlin he confided that he had played it in private to his musician friends, adding: 'I can't tell you how impressed these brave Teutons are by this brilliant fantasia, so new and so amusing.' In the end it was the pianist Madeleine Jaeger who gave the *Bourrée* its first public performance in Paris in 1893.

The *Bourrée*, however, was not the only work for the piano that Chabrier wrote during the last years of his life; and it is time now to mention the *Cinq pièces*, composed in the same years as the *Bourrée* but published posthumously. These, though very different in character, and incidentally, far less well known, reveal yet another side of Chabrier's instinctive sympathy for and skill in writing for the piano. In these *Cinq pièces posthumes*, entitled respectively: *Aubade, Ballabile, Caprice, Feuillet d'album* and *Ronde champêtre*, the composer is gay and tender, humorous, idyllic and boisterous by turn; and though on a small scale, sometimes bordering even on the 'salon' style, *à la* Chaminade, the pieces are delightful to play and deserve to be better known.[1] It is interesting to compare with these late pieces the early *Impromptu* (1873) dedicated to Mme Manet, which was Chabrier's first piano work of any importance and already bore the stamp of his highly original and personal style. (*See* Chapter One, page 8.)

We come now to the work to which above all others Chabrier, during the last years of his life, was most passionately attached and which indeed became almost an obsession with him as he strove to complete it before his illness and failing faculties made it impossible for him to realize his dream. It was in 1888 that he first formed the project of writing an opera on a libretto which Catulle Mendès had based on Goethe's story of *The Bride of Corinth*, taking as the title the name of the heroine, *Briséis*. It was to his friend van Dyck that he first revealed his intention in the spring of that year, and in a letter dated 1st August, written from his country retreat, he gave van Dyck some further information about the work he had in mind. Describing it as 'a paraphrase in three acts and four tableaux of Goethe's legend', he thought at that time that it would mean for him fifteen or sixteen months of very hard work.

I'll do my very best; no need to tell you that it will be ultra-modern [*d'un moderne à tout casser*] and that there will be neither a chorus of bathing belles nor any triumphal marches.

In any case, there's no danger of that with Mendès—serious
theatre is the only kind he understands. Naturally I'm setting
it to music which will be very much my own; I don't know
whether it will be French, but it most certainly will not be
German; my first duty, after all, is to my own country! I try
to inoculate myself with the *aesthetics* of the man of bronze,
but emphatically not with his music, because *that belongs to
him*, and one should never rob anyone, even if one has to stay
poor (but honest) oneself. . . . I shall be staying down here
indefinitely for I want to get on as fast as possible with
Briséis. . . .

As it turned out, months went by before Chabrier had written a
note, although he still professed himself enchanted with the
subject—to the surprise of his friends, it should be added, as at
first sight nothing could have seemed less suited to his particular
temperamental make-up and reputation as a musical humorist
than this story, set in Corinth in the first century A.D., of the
young girl Briséis, whose conversion to Christianity to save her
aged mother prevents her from finding happiness with her young
pagan lover.

The letters he wrote to his friends, his family, his publishers
and his librettists between 1889 and 1892 make sad reading.
His determination to make *Briséis* his crowning achievement, the
work by which he would always be remembered—'I'm treating
it as my own flesh and blood, I want it to be *superfine*'—was
continually being thwarted by his awareness of his failing powers,
and by long periods of discouragement when he felt unable to
work. It was during one of these fits of depression that he wrote
to his wife:

For the last week I haven't done a thing; I've nothing in my
head—I'm in one of my bad phases, so you can imagine what
a state I'm in! No matter how hard I try, I haven't written a
note, not a single note, all the week. What a life! And you
aren't there . . . You've no idea how difficult it is, this blasted

Briséis! It's nowhere near finished yet, I can promise you that! I don't want it to send me dotty, that's why I shall be obliged to lay off for a while and then come back to this long and complicated job. . . .

He was constantly having trouble, too, with his librettists—for Mendès had co-opted a young symbolist poet, Ephraïm Mikhaël (who was to die before Chabrier, in 1890 at the age of twenty-four) to help him with the libretto—much to the annoyance of Chabrier, who was constantly complaining of this young man's dilatoriness and failure to answer letters, bombarding his publishers with his complaints, and protesting that it was too much to expect him to come up to Paris from the country every time he had a point to discuss with his librettists:

I wrote yesterday to Mikhaël to tell him he was playing the fool with me, but I've had no reply this morning. I consider the incident closed, but at this rate and in view of the inexplicable bad faith shown by my collaborators with whom I have always been very correct, *Briséis* is likely to be on the stocks for a long while yet. . . . And she'll have to stay there, more's the pity. . . . How will all this end? Shall we come to some understanding? And then no doubt it will all begin again after a few months; it's much more serious than you think, and I'm more and more worried by the feeling that I'm not getting the support I need and that I can't rely on my collaborators. (Tiénot; from an autograph letter to Enoch.)

And when, finally, thanks to the intervention of his publishers, he did get a reply from Mikhaël, he complained that even then the text he had asked for was not forthcoming, and suggested that in future he would ask his publishers to carry out any corrections he might want to make, for after all *Briséis* was their property: this would be the best solution.

What does emerge from all this correspondence is the infinite trouble Chabrier was prepared to take over his libretto, and his highly professional approach to every little problem that arose.

For example, he wrote to Mendès asking him to take another look at a certain passage at the end of the first scene in the first act where he wasn't very happy about what he called

> a little dodge *à la Scribe* which no doubt you're not very pleased with yourself; I mean where Hylas says: 'Let us repeat the oath...' Would it not be possible to delete this 'let us repeat', and to lengthen the verse (I don't mind that) in a more poetic way ... it ought to be possible to introduce the oath again (I feel strongly about this) without *announcing* it in this rather naïve fashion. ... Do see to this, my dear friend, and send me your little readjustment as soon as possible. ...

In another letter to Mendès Chabrier is concerned about a question of stage management and makes the following very pertinent points (Pincherle, 1939):

> At the beginning of the second act the girls (in the chorus)— just like the sailors in the first act—start to sing in the wings and enter from the *right*. What I mean is, this is too much of a repetition, and I can't plan my music unless I know whether you really *want* them to come on in the same way as the sailors, or would you have any objection to the girls being already on stage when the curtain rises, or coming on *almost immediately*? Whatever we decide, my music *cannot be the same*, so it's essential for me to know. Moreover, the chorus in the wings never comes over well, and no one would hear the words ('une brise heureuse', etc. ...) which are charming here, and as I have already said, this would be the same *mise en scène*, at any rate the musical *mise en scène* as in the first act. Then again, my deaconesses will make their entry very much in the same way; —fortunately, however (we altered this the other day), they sing on stage and go off while the orchestra is playing. All you have to do, then, my friend, is to drop me a line to say: 'Very well, then; you can have them singing on stage *to start with*'— and that's all I want. You see those three words by return of post won't take much of your time. ...

In another letter Chabrier is at pains to point out to Mendès that, whereas in poetry the same *rhythm* can be used to express any sentiment or emotion, in music this is not possible, as any alteration in the mood of a musical phrase—from sad to gay, for example—must affect its shape and rhythm. This concern with the finer points of prosody and the marriage of words to music is evidence that Chabrier's mind was no less attuned to the niceties of literary composition than was his ear to those of music or his eye to the refinements of the painter's art. In this he resembled Debussy and Ravel; but such an enlightened aesthetic appreciation and understanding of the relation between the verbal, aural and visual arts was the exception rather than the rule among nineteenth-century French musicians.

It seems nevertheless pathetic, even tragic, that Chabrier should have worn himself out in the last years of his life in a supreme effort to achieve what he hoped would be his masterpiece, while failing to see that neither the theme of *Briséis* nor its treatment in the libretto concocted by Mendès and Mikhaël was at all suitable as a vehicle for the expression of his own very individual and unconventional musical personality. Although his gifts, as we have seen, lay in quite another direction—in a sphere to which he could make, and did make, a very valuable and unique contribution—he was unfortunately obsessed by a desire to write grand operas instead of being content to be supreme in the field in which he excelled—light opera. In any case, the choice of *Briséis* as a subject seems very strange, and it is hard to understand why he should have been attracted by this rather unpleasing story of a selfish old woman forcing her daughter to ruin her life by embracing the Christian faith merely in order to save her mother's life.

There are five scenes in the first act (the only one to be completed). In the first we hear the sailors who are to be Hylas's companions on the trading expedition which he hopes will make him rich enough to marry Briséis, singing as they prepare their boats. Hylas serenades Briséis and throws flowers up to her window. In

Scene ii the lovers proclaim their love in an impassioned duet and swear to be faithful to one another, come what may. In the third scene Thanasto, the mother, racked by pain, invokes Christ and swears to devote her life, if she is spared, to spreading the new faith among her people. She collapses in a faint and is carried off by her retainers. In the scene that follows Briséïs and her attendant women pray to Apollo, but are interrupted by the appearance of the Catechist, carrying a cross, who prays and chants a litany to the Saviour who alone could cure the sorely stricken Thanasto. He is mocked by Stratokles, the head man of the Thanasto household, who blasphemes against the new religion of the Christians, but Briséïs implores the Catechist to tell her if his God could save her mother. He replies that if she will follow him and embrace the Christian faith, her mother will be cured. Briséïs, torn between her devotion to Thanasto and her love for Hylas (whom she can never marry if she becomes a Christian) hesitates, but in the final scene Thanasto insists that the only way she can save her mother's life is to renounce her pagan faith; only thus can the vow Thanasto has made to lead her daughter to God be fulfilled. Briséïs in despair consents, and the exulting Thanasto celebrates her victory in a paean of praise to the Almighty.

Out of this farrago of religiosity, romanticism, heroics and hysteria Chabrier has nevertheless contrived to construct an act which contains some memorable music—notably the austerely simple and quasi-modal declamation allotted to the Catechist, some eloquent and effective choruses and moments of lyricism in the dialogue of the lovers. But the score is over-elaborate and the emotional atmosphere overheated; and over it all one is only too conscious—notably more so than in *Gwendoline*—of the portentous shadow of Richard Wagner. There are even passages in which the introduction of Wagnerian harmonies and progressions almost amounts to plagiarism—though, to be fair, there are others where Chabrier exhibits his own unmistakable brand of adventurous originality. He was certainly conscious up to a point of adopting Wagnerian procedures, though, as we have seen, he always insisted that he only wanted to write music that would be strictly his own. But in a letter to his friend Lecocq he admitted that composing *Briséis* according to Wagnerian principles was very hard work:

> . . . you'll understand what a long, meticulous and difficult job it is to 'leitmotiver' [*sic*] the orchestra throughout without declamation . . . with 'leitmotifs' that have been heard already in full and that have to be twisted and tortured and repeated over and over again . . . this gives me a lot of trouble, and obviously contributes greatly to the unity of the work as a whole, but since I want clarity above all I assure you I have to work at it like a slave . . .

There is no doubt that Chabrier saw himself as a pioneer so far as opera in France was concerned, and in the same letter to Lecocq he was already looking into the future:

> . . . there won't be any going backwards, in my opinion, and in the matter of what is known as lyric drama I wonder what they'll be doing in 1950, because art is perfectible, and there is no doubt that the general level of the works we're aiming at is higher, our ideals more ambitious and the importance we attach to the orchestra more evident than in works like *Les Huguenots*, *La Juive*, *Robert*, etc., which I'm far from despising, you mustn't think that, and which I should have been proud to have written in 1832; but there's no doubt about it— Wagner has put an end to all that and we've got to go forward —it's inevitable.

Chabrier was now living practically all the year round in Touraine and constantly writing letters to his friends or his publishers either about his state of health, which was steadily deteriorating, or about his beloved *Briséis* on which he continued to work as long as he was able, although he never succeeded, after he had finished the first act, in getting on to paper more than some rough sketches for the remaining acts. He had hoped that Vincent d'Indy would accept the task of completing his unfinished score, and after his death his elder son, Marcel, asked d'Indy whether he would be willing to do what his father had so much desired. Not surprisingly d'Indy felt unable to undertake what would have been an impossible task, and wrote a long and tactful letter to Marcel explaining why he could not accept this responsibility. The text of his letter, now part of the Don Chabrier collection in the Bibliothèque Nationale, is dated 5th October 1894 (less than a month after Chabrier's death) and is as follows (Tiénot):

My dear Marcel,

You know how deep was my affection for your dear father, and so I hope you will not think badly of me when I tell you quite frankly and as a friend that I could not possibly make myself responsible for completing *Briséis*. When your poor father asked me last December to 'help him' to orchestrate *Briséis*, I replied that I would gladly do so, knowing well that at that time he was incapable of working and that this meant that I would have at least two acts to orchestrate (a year or eighteen months' work); but, naturally, I told him I would only do the orchestration and have nothing to do with the composition, as this would be impossible for me for artistic and temperamental reasons. At that time I had no idea of the state the work was in, and when I was able to see for myself (last April when I saw poor Emmanuel for the last time) that the work was not even *half sketched out*, I hadn't the heart, in the presence of those *two* sick people (for your mother was then undoubtedly ill herself), to disappoint them by flatly refusing, as perhaps I should have done, to take on this work; and as your father was always saying: 'but I thought I had written more than that . . . someone must have lost my manuscript . . .' I said to him: 'Well, then, try and find what you have written down and sketch in what is missing; then I promise you I will orchestrate the whole thing, even if the notes are only sketched in, provided, of course, that *the music is all there.*' Your mother can testify that those were my very words. But the music *is not all there*, and in my opinion never will be, for I ask you, what musician could possibly assimilate completely a temperament so impulsive, so original and so unexpected as that of your poor father . . . I consider it an offence against art for anyone to complete a work left unfinished by a serious musician if this means he has got to put something of *himself* into it. If it were only a question of orchestration, that would be like repairing a damaged fresco, slightly reprehensible perhaps, but a possible and sometimes useful undertaking; but to draw on one's own resources and try to combine them with those of another and totally different nature will never produce anything but a hybrid mixture and, in any case, a negative artistic result. For it means, if you can understand what I'm saying, dear friend, that either the artist appointed to complete the work will make it entirely his own—in other words nothing, or almost nothing, of the original sketches will remain, and in that case the style of this work will be so different from that of other of the dead artist's works that it can hardly be considered his; or, alternatively, if the adapter tries honestly to assimilate the style and temperament of the other, to copy his forms and reproduce his formulae, then there'll be no spontaneous invention, nothing but a simple copy devoid of interest, a work devoid of art. In either case I think the result is undesirable, and if only on account of my friendship with poor Chabrier I would feel obliged to refuse to be party to a profanation of his work which could only result in either my enriching myself with his ideas (and in any case I could not possibly work on Mendès's text) or else in the creation of a formless artistic mass totally lacking in harmony, the first essential of all art. . . . It would distress me if *Briséïs* were completed; what there is of it can perfectly well be played and sung at concerts and in this way will arouse great interest. . . . I hope, my dear friend, that you will not be offended by my refusal, whatever anyone may say, because I can assure you that very few people have loved your poor father and his works as much as I have; and whenever there's any question of putting his works forward and making them known where they are not known already I will certainly do this, just as I have done in the past.

As if to confirm what d'Indy predicted, *Briséïs* was in fact first performed in public at a Lamoureux concert on 31st January 1897; it was not until the spring of 1899 that it was finally produced at the Paris Opéra. Enthusiastically received in the concert hall it apparently failed to make quite the same impression at the Opéra. The critic of *La Petite République*, for example, thought the Opéra would have done better to revive *Gwendoline* rather than put on an incomplete work interrupted by the death of its composer, and dismissed the whole venture as 'a completely useless demonstration'. He thought it would fail to win as full a recognition of Chabrier's genius as a revival of *Gwendoline* would have done, and was not likely to appeal greatly to opera goers—and in this he was right, for *Briséïs* on this occasion ran for only six nights. It was well known, he added, that Chabrier was distressed that, while *Gwendoline* had been acclaimed in Germany, it had been neglected in his own country; and this would have been a good opportunity to redress the balance. It is interesting to note, before taking leave of *Briséïs*, that, as in the case of *Gwendoline*, it was actually in Germany that it had its first stage performance before it reached Paris, having been produced at the Theatre Royal in Berlin, under Richard Strauss, in January 1899, four months before its Paris *première*. It was revived at the Paris Opéra, apparently for the last time, in 1916.

Chabrier, of course, did not live to see *Briséïs* performed, but at the end of his life he did have the satisfaction of having his *Gwendoline* at last accepted by the Paris Opéra and of being present at the first performance in the sad circumstances already described (page 65).[2] By now the general paralysis from which he suffered had made recovery impossible, and on 13th September

1894, in his fifty-fourth year, he died. He was buried, not in the cemetery at Passy, near his friend Manet, as he would have wished, but, owing to lack of space, at Montparnasse. In his funeral oration, pronounced over the grave, Victorin de Joncières, an old friend of Chabrier's and President of the Société des Auteurs et Compositeurs Dramatiques, spoke of 'the works whose sincerity, originality, forcefulness and emotional content ensure for your memory the admiration due to one of the most eminent masters of French music'.

A few years after Emmanuel's death, his widow, who apparently suffered from the same affliction, also died; and by 1914, with the death at the age of thirty-seven of the younger son André (Marcel had died aged thirty-six in 1910) the direct line of Emmanuel Chabrier was extinct. Today there still lives in Chabrier's native town of Ambert, in the Puy-de-Dôme, a distant relative, a descendant of Jean-Baptiste Chabrier (b. 1772), the eldest brother of Chabrier's grandfather, Claude-Marie Alexis (b. 1779).

It was not until 1912 that, on the initiative of the late Joseph Desaymard (to whom we owe the invaluable collection of Chabrier's letters from which I have freely quoted in the course of this book), a monument to the composer was erected in his native town. It was surmounted by a bust of Chabrier executed by the Belgian sculptor Constantin Meunier (1831–1905), and the following year an enlarged version of this bust was placed on Chabrier's tomb in the cemetery at Montparnasse. These public celebrations in honour of Chabrier brought a flood of tributes from musicians who knew and admired his work expressed in the warmest terms as the following extracts will show:

From Charles Lamoureux: 'Emmanuel Chabrier, the unforgettable friend, has left in his works the deep imprint of his mind and heart. His lively originality, overflowing gaiety, his kindness, his tenderness and his enthusiastic nature are exhibited in dazzling colours on his musical palette, and the first act of *Briséis* showed what we were entitled to expect from a great artist whose independence, convictions and upright nature never made concessions to fashion or convention.'

From Ernest Chausson: 'Chabrier possessed in the highest degree that gift which makes great artists, and through which they re-create everything—a strong personality. . . . This originality, which constituted his genius, was also the cause of the peculiar charm which emanated from him and which only survives in the memory of those who knew and loved him. And that is why while so many voices will be heard in praise of his works I have wished simply to recall the happy hours spent in his company which none of his friends will forget.'

From Vincent d'Indy: 'A poet, and above all the poet of sounds, the musician, can only create through the heart; art cannot live without feeling. With Emmanuel Chabrier, that great primitive (and here I speak as a friend who will always have for him a deep affection), everything stemmed from the heart: that is why Chabrier was a great artist.'

From André Messager: 'By the strength of his character, the irresistible force of his inspiration, the novelty of his rhythms, the originality of his ideas, Chabrier deserves a place among the leading musicians of the modern French school. An artist inspired by the noblest ideals, always aiming at the highest perfection, he made from his heart music that touches the heart. . . . His inspiration is like a rushing torrent sweeping all before it; and if sometimes it carries earth and stones, it also contains the purest gold. . . .'

From Felix Mottl: 'I consider the works of Emmanuel Chabrier to occupy a very important place in the history of music. The gracefulness of his invention, intensity of feeling and technical

mastery ensure for him a place among composers who should
have earned the admiration of the entire world of music. I hope
and am confident that this hour of justice will arrive, and I shall
then be proud to have been one of those who, beyond the frontiers
of his native country, helped to win recognition for his rare gifts
as a creative artist.'

Finally, in 1924 public recognition of Chabrier took the form
of a petition to the Municipality to name a street in Paris after
him—a petition signed by all the most eminent musicians in
France, including Ravel, Roussel, d'Indy, Cortot, Duparc,
Bruneau, Dukas, Pierné, Florent Schmitt, Reynaldo Hahn,
Messager, Ropartz and Samazeuilh, and the painter Claude
Monet. The result may be seen today in the Square Emmanuel
Chabrier in the Batignolles district of the seventeenth *arrondisse-
ment*, not far from the Avenue Trudaine where Chabrier lived
when in Paris during the last years of his life, and where he died.

CHAPTER NINE

The man and his music—His Letters and his friends.

IF Emmanuel Chabrier had not been born, would it have been necessary to invent him? If we believe that he and he alone introduced into French music an element, a quality, that we find nowhere else expressed in so pure and so concentrated a form, then the answer is yes. Throughout the ages it could be said that French music had oscillated between extremes of intellectualism on the one hand and triviality on the other. Between the solemn music of Machaut and the *salon* music of Chaminade, the rigour of Rameau and the ribaldry of the Bouffes-Parisiens, there had been little but a soft core of sugar and sentimentality in the theatre and a too-facile acceptance of religious formulae in the organ-loft. These sweeping generalizations, for all their superficiality, nevertheless serve to pinpoint the fact that in French music, generally speaking, the best music has tended to be too literary and perhaps self-consciously 'artistic', and the worst too merely ear-tickling and frivolous. In the seventeenth and eighteenth centuries the cleavage lay mainly between the Court and the market-place; in the nineteenth between an intellectual and artistic *élite* and the bourgeoisie. Between the 'highbrows' and the man-in-the-street there was a vacuum that needed to be filled; and it could well be that Chabrier was sent into the world to perform just that function.

An acute and perceptive contemporary critic, M. Stanislas Fumet (1946), writing on Chabrier on the occasion of the centenary of his birth, suggested that the time had come for a new approach altogether to what he called the 'phénomène Chabrier'—a composer who wrote music that, in his view, was the very prototype of 'French music that had not made any mistakes'. The implication here is that he was contrasting Chabrier's music with that of the intellectual school who were supposed by critics and public alike to be operating on a higher artistic level, but who were all the same open to the criticism that their work was possibly a shade too sophisticated and consciously 'artistic'. From any suspicion of this Chabrier's music was certainly free, and therein, in the opinion of the writer, lay its great merit. Something of the same order of ideas was undoubtedly in the minds of 'Les Six' when they reproached Ravel with what they called his 'écriture artiste'—a reproach somewhat maliciously intensified by Satie when he said that Ravel put in all the punctuation but forgot to write anything underneath. The 'Six', incidentally, were among the first to resuscitate Chabrier after he had undergone an unjust period of eclipse and, as M. Fumet points out, being intelligent musicians, what had probably attracted them to him in the first place was the fact that 'he had not waited for them to be an intelligent musician himself'.

Chabrier, in fact, was both an intelligent and an instinctive musician—a rare phenomenon. His was an unselfconscious art; he was, as it were, a channel for pure music which flowed through him but remained always under his control. He wrote, as d'Indy and others had observed, 'from the heart', but there was nothing sloppy or sentimental about his inspiration; and the fact that writing music, as we have seen, did not come easily to him was one reason why he always maintained a critical attitude towards his own work, setting himself high standards and making no concessions that ran counter to his principles. If it be true, as M. Fumet suggests, that France, 'which knows how to think musically had lost the habit of feeling musically', then it was Chabrier's mission to redress the balance; and because he did this so successfully his place in the annals of French music is assured. He was, in fact, the best composer of the best type of so-called 'light music' there has ever been; and he was this because he was also a highly proficient, and above all extremely intelligent, all-round musician who tended to look upon the conventional distinction between 'light' and 'serious' music as fundamentally untenable.[1] He expressed this clearly in a letter he wrote towards the end

of his life to his friend the tenor van Dyck in a passage that is
worth quoting, expressing as it does Chabrier's rational attitude
to the whole question of '*genres*' in music.

Great art can be *gay* as well as *tragic*; you can have the
Meistersinger and you can have *Tristan*. But it is generally
agreed that *great art* must be tragic—and if the *Meistersinger*
didn't exist I should find it hard to name a single 'gay' work
treated as seriously, so far as actual workmanship is concerned,
as any ordinary opera. Beckmesser is quite as much a creation
of genius as any other more 'serious' character in the Wagnerian repertory; and laughter is no less valid than tears. To laugh
or to cry—there's nothing else; and Wagner wanted here to
have a good laugh and, I must say, succeeded marvellously in
this absolutely extraordinary work which I know, almost by
heart, both words and music, from beginning to end.

Well now—forgive me, all you great masters and men of
genius, if I talk about myself—what I want to say is this: that
this idiotic little *Roi malgré lui* is much more *polished* and better
put together in its category of *French opéra-comique* than works
classed as operas or grand operas such as *Bélisaire*, *Excelsior*,
Mireille, *Jean Chevalier*, *Philémon* and a heap of others including
Fra Diavolo.[2] And so, *without demeaning itself*, the Vienna
Imperial Opera might very well produce *Le Roi*. It's not a
question of consigning a work to the waste-paper basket,
without examining it, on the grounds that it's not an opera!
They have swallowed the whole of Delibes and feathered their
nest with him, so *Le Roi* might suit them very well—all the
more so because, as I told you in my letter the other day, they
were pretending they had had enough of *opera-seria* so might be
glad to have something gay. . . .

Chabrier was always very critical of current musical fashions in
Paris where, he wrote on another occasion to van Dyck:

Art with a capital letter, serious art, is bogged down and
stagnating. At the Opéra Gounod and La Patti are exhibiting

themselves and coining money; Massenet is conducting
rehearsals of *Esclarmonde* at the Opéra-Comique and Saint-
Saëns doing the same with *Ascanio* at the Opéra; Godard is
churning out a *Dante*: all this is very far from being great
Art. . . . d'Indy is engaged on a big work, but it'll take him
another couple of years to finish! Lamoureux is doing nothing;
the concerts are now only a family affair; there's no longer
any choir, and hardly any singing. He's making money and
just jogging along . . . contentedly serving up the old pro-
grammes, and the public flocks to hear them. The time for
any serious effort is past; *Lohengrin* just about finished him
off . . . all this strictly between ourselves, of course. . . .[3]

The above quotations show, among other things, that while
Chabrier was undoubtedly in essence an 'instinctive' musician,
this did not prevent him from being an extremely intelligent
one. He knew very well what was going on around him, and he
could see the faults, the excesses and the deficiencies of his
colleagues and contemporaries; but when he was writing music
himself he obeyed only his own instincts. Like a strong swimmer
who feels at home in the sea, Chabrier when immersed in music
felt he was in his own element, plunging and diving to bring up
whatever treasures he might encounter, untroubled by any conventions or preconceived theories which might cramp his style.
In this way he made discoveries and innovations which were
entirely spontaneous and not due to any conscious intellectual
exploration. His was a musical talent of the 'purest' kind, with
no admixture of rationalization; his delight in rhythmic and
harmonic ingenuities, bold modulations and occasional unexpected dissonances, was typical of his exuberant, uninhibited
temperament; and in addition he possessed, to a degree rare
among musicians, not only a robust sense of humour but a lively
and caustic wit as well. It was this humorous vein that runs
through so much of his music that caused his great friend Vincent
d'Indy to nickname him 'l'ange du cocasse' (the angel of the

absurd—an allusion, no doubt, to Poe's 'ange du bizarre'). For
d'Indy, Chabrier was 'le musicien cocasse par excellence . . .
everything in his music is unexpected' and, although he never
consciously aims at raising a laugh, 'humour and drollery sprang
from his pen because he was made like that and could not write
otherwise—it was his natural "tournure d'esprit"—so natural
that he often did not suspect himself how irresistibly comic
certain passages were in his music; and when one pointed them
out to him he would laugh at his own drollery'. d'Indy pays
generous tribute to the personality of Emmanuel Chabrier,
'exquisite from every point of view'. He had no enemies, and in
dealings with others he never showed any trace of jealousy or envy:

> We find everywhere in his life as in his works examples of
> effusion, emotion, gentleness and tenderness without senti-
> mentality, rare enough among musicians today. . . . What
> is remarkable in Chabrier is that the qualities of tenderness
> and exuberance are so inextricably linked in his music that
> it would be impossible to tone down one without harming the
> other. And it is that, in my opinion, that constitutes his
> undeniable originality.

d'Indy does not share the view that Chabrier was really a 'precursor' of the new movement in music, but was inevitably
affected by it, since it was a time when 'harmony, aggregations
of sonorities and what is sometimes called "harmonic counter-
point" (an expression which I defy any *musician* to explain) are
the only qualities admired today'. He described Chabrier as
primarily a melodist, deplored (as we saw in a previous chapter)
his obsession with grand opera, but admired wholeheartedly
L'Etoile: 'A little masterpiece of comic music as brilliant as the
Barber and without doubt much funnier and more musical than
all the operettas that came before or after it.' Rather surprisingly,
especially in view of his enthusiastic appreciation of it at the time
(*see* Chapter Six, page 74) d'Indy in this paper calls *Le Roi
malgré lui* 'une opérette lugubre'—but gives no reason for this

judgment. The choice of epithet, in this context especially, seems very strange.[4]

It would be easy to point to weaknesses in Chabrier's music apparent here and there—e.g. his tendency to overwork certain melodic and harmonic clichés, such as doubling a melody at the octave and the use, at cadences, of a little descending *gruppetto* derived from the notes of the dominant chord—e.g. (in the key of C) B A F D C—which occurs over and over again in his piano works. Occasionally too he is capable of approaching perilously near the borders of *salon* music, but generally saves himself in time by some unexpected and entirely characteristic harmonic or melodic twist. As regards the extent to which he was 'influenced' by Wagner, this we have seen was more in the realm of theory than practice, although it was no doubt the reason for his obsession with the theatre and his mistaken conviction that his true vocation lay in the field of grand opera. In point of fact, of course, as we know now, his best works owe nothing whatsoever to Wagner or any other foreign influence, but everything to his own unique personality and essential and even exaggerated 'Frenchness'. One has only to think of the three masterly operettas —*L'Etoile*, *Une Education manquée* and *Le Roi malgré lui*; all the piano works, especially the *Pièces pittoresques*, the *Bourrée* and the *Trois valses romantiques* for two pianos; *La Sulamite*; *Ode à la musique* and *España*; the inimitable 'farmyard' set of songs and a handful of other songs, such as *Chanson pour Jeanne*, *Les Cigales*, *Toutes les fleurs* and the delightfully mischievous *Lied*, with words by Catulle Mendès, published posthumously. There is, however, a slightly 'drawing-room' flavour about some of these songs for voice and piano, except the farmyard set which sparkle with wit and sly fun-poking and have something of Satie's 'dead-pan' humour. *Gwendoline* and *Briséïs* are in a class apart; they cannot be dismissed as unimportant because both contain some fine and effective music, but one feels that in them Chabrier is 'out of character', and putting an undue strain on his natural temperament and talents.

One thing that needs to be stressed in any critical estimation of his *œuvre* as a whole is the high level of workmanship and technical proficiency (including expert orchestration) it reveals which, in view of the fact that he was basically an autodidact who took up music professionally late in life and never acquired that 'facility' that many lesser artists possess, is certainly remarkable. He may perhaps have been one of those who have more genius than talent; but whatever his deficiencies may have been, it was sheer force of temperament that earned for him his distinctive place in the annals of French music. For the impact he made on the world of music in the last quarter of the nineteenth century was like a gust of wind sweeping through the musty corridors of some imposing but neglected palace, blowing away the cobwebs and the dust and reinvigorating the air. This is not to imply that Chabrier was a greater or more important composer than many of his contemporaries, but merely that he was *different*. He snapped his fingers at schools and conventions, theories and cliques and wrote uninhibitedly the kind of music that corresponded to his own temperament and that was just as much a part of himself as any other of his appetites. It may well be argued that other composers have done the same, but few have been so little influenced by fashion or tradition as Chabrier.

It is important to remember that the kind of 'Establishment' with which Chabrier found himself confronted when he emerged from his long apprenticeship as a musical amateur and very junior civil servant, without ever having passed through the Conservatoire or any other official teaching establishment, was dominated on the one hand by César Franck and his followers, including the young d'Indy, and on the other by composers, to mention no others, of such standing as Saint-Saëns, Gounod, Duparc, Chausson, Bizet and Massenet. (Chabrier died about the time when Debussy was making his first impact, and Ravel was still a student.) But by sheer force of character and a determination to be a composer and serve music he gradually came to the fore,

and with the production of his first operetta, *L'Etoile*, his contemporaries were forced to admit that a new star had arisen who
would have to be reckoned with.

What manner of man, then, was he—this stocky, ebullient
little Auvergnat who thus elbowed his way, so to speak, into the
inner circles of this late nineteenth-century Parisian musical
confraternity and soon became accepted as 'one of them'? Short
of stature, portly and with a comfortable homespun look about
him, with his round head and short arms and legs, he had the
typical physique of the inhabitants of his native province of
Auvergne. And yet, having migrated to the capital at an early
age, he rapidly became Parisianized and developed into a curious
mixture of bourgeois, Bohemian and boulevardier rolled into
one. He adored the life and bustle of Montmartre (within or
near whose frontiers he made his three Parisian homes, rue
Mosnier, rue Rochechouart and Avenue Trudaine), and was
equally at home in the more fashionable district of the Opéra
and the Grands Boulevards. He was at the same time, as we
have seen, a family man, devoted to his wife and sons; and he
had a large circle of friends and apparently no enemies. Overflowing with vitality and an enormous zest for living, he appreciated the good things of life, physical as well as intellectual, and
expressed himself in the most picturesque and sometimes
Rabelaisian language interlarding his conversation with exclamations such as 'Eh, bonnes gens! . . . mon gaillard . . mon cocotin',
fond of a good story and good company and hating shams and
snobbery. As a letter-writer he excelled, wielding a most felicitous
pen and showing a real feeling for style.[5] His writing, like his
conversation, was laced with a profusion of racy slang (sometimes difficult to translate) with an occasional harmless hint of
bawdiness and, running through it all, an extraordinary warmth
and exuberant vitality. It is fortunate that so many of his letters
have been preserved, as they provide us with a portrait of the man
no less eloquent than those painted by his great friend Manet.
Perhaps the most attractive of all the traits in his character

was his fundamental simplicity and utter lack of snobbishness or pretension of any kind. The essential goodness and kind-heartedness of the man are nowhere more touchingly reflected than in the countless letters he wrote all through his life to his beloved old nurse, Nanine, to whom he was devoted. After the stroke she had suffered, which had left her partly paralysed, he would write to her regularly, though far from well himself, not only regaling her with family gossip and details of his everyday life, but keeping her informed about his work and people he had met, and encouraging her to keep her spirits up in the knowledge that she was not forgotten. The following are extracts from letters written from the Chabriers' country house in Touraine in the spring and summer of 1890:

> The weather is still deplorable; I can't send you anything from the garden, my poor dear; the flowers are all squashed down, the paths all muddy—it's pitiful and boring in the extreme. But I'm working hard, and my work—though I can't say it's *progressing*, for there's a lot to do yet before it's finished —is nevertheless getting on slowly. I'm rather like my poor old nanny at the moment, always sitting down [Nanine was confined to a wheelchair since her stroke] and always alone, because at meals I'm always so absorbed in my musical cal-culations that I often don't listen to what Granny [his mother-in-law] is saying. In any case, that doesn't upset her, and she goes on chattering as if I were all ears. . . . My great distraction is our asparagus! It doesn't grow very fast in this weather, and bunches are small and expensive. But it lasts for so short a time that I try and eat as much as I can while it lasts. . . .

On another occasion he sends her an amusing description of the local village band:

La Membrolle, 30 May 1890.

My dear little Nanon,

We've got some flowers at last and this morning we wanted

to send you some. But you've got all the boxes there were in the house, because we didn't know where to put them. As for strawberries and cherries, not a sign of any! We had absolutely nothing in the way of dessert for lunch—it's shocking. . . . In Tours they're very expensive—2f.50 a pound for strawberries and 1f.25 for cherries. One's never known such a late season. . . . On Sunday there's a big procession, with wayside shrines and first communion for the children . . . the band is already rehearsing; in the evening, coming from the cottage windows, I can hear humble trombones and prudent saxhorns emitting a few disjointed notes here and there that remind one of the hoarse intermittent croaking of a distant toad. It's hideous enough like that; but when they're all playing together it's really horrible. . . . We'll be seeing you soon . . .

Your old Mavel who loves you very much.

In another letter he will be telling her about his goldfinches: 'I've got a pair now, husband and wife; I've just bought a little nest for them—it's up to them to find out what to do with it . . .' or about how he washed the little rabbit all over till it turned scarlet, about what they had for dinner, about what Mme X said to Mme Y—all this out of the goodness of his heart and in the middle of his work, just to keep the old lady amused and make her feel she was still a part of the family. Even when he went abroad on business he would not forget to write to his Nanine— one day from Geneva where he had gone for an important musical occasion, on another from Munich where he had been invited to attend the first performance in that town of his opera *Gwendoline*, and so on; wherever he might be he liked always to keep in touch. Thus we find him writing to her from Paris on the eve of his departure for Munich to tell her that Saint-Saëns had been to dine with him: 'He was charming and we passed a very pleasant evening together *tête-à-tête*. We gave him a chicken and a steak with artichokes, but he hardly eats anything. . . .'

Apart from music and family affairs Chabrier rarely commented on politics or events in the outside world; but in 1891, when General Boulanger committed suicide on the tomb of his mistress (Marguerite Crouzet) he wrote to a relative: 'And what about Boulanger? He made his exit like an 1830 Romantic—decidedly not very manly. Imagine our Napoleon blowing his brains out! Not likely! Oh well; so long as he's found his Marguerite, so much the better for them.'

We have already touched on Chabrier's many-sided interests apart from music, and especially as a connoisseur of painting. In literature too he knew his way about, and was something of a collector of rare books, keeping an eye on publishers' catalogues, especially those of Léon Vanier, who specialized in the 'decadents', or what we should now probably call the *avant-garde*. Thus, only three years before his death, he wrote as follows to Vanier asking him to send a batch of books he had seen advertised in *Le Figaro*, one of which was a new work by Verlaine. He specified that he wanted them as soon as they were published (first editions only), adding: 'If the book by Verlaine, an old friend of mine for twenty-five years, comes out this month, please ask him to write something for me on the front page.' (The expression he used was 'mettre sa forte patte'.) [6]

It took Chabrier some time to live down his reputation as an 'amateur', as we have seen; in reality his approach to the technical side of his art, down to the smallest details, was always highly professional. He attached the greatest importance to the exact observance, in the interpretation of his own works, of every nuance of expression, *tempo*, dynamics and the like, which he was very careful to mark with great precision and expected his interpreters to observe as strictly as he did himself. In the days when he was working as assistant to the conductor Lamoureux he must have had to handle many scores submitted by budding and other composers; and it was doubtless his recollection of his experiences at that time that caused him in later life to express his views on this subject in no uncertain terms in a letter to his

friend, the composer Charles Lecocq, to whom it would appear
that he had submitted some MS., or perhaps a proof for correc-
tion. Dated La Membrolle, 8th December 1891, the letter ran
as follows:

Thank you, my dear Lecocq, my dear friend; you've really
been kindness itself and, what's more, you are always right!
I've corrected everything, even the question marks; anyway,
you are certainly one of the 'clean' ones, as I call them; I've
a horror of bunglers and botchers, and I could mention a few
of those who have never even put a *tempo* mark in their MSS.,
nor a *ritardando*, nor a *forte* or anything at all. They are the
dirty dogs who never *clean up* their scores, symphonies or
whatever! And so when this stuff reaches the players' desks,
you should just see the conductor's expression! Ah!, but—
someone will object—today composers are 'cleaner' in this
way than they used to be. . . . Maybe, but I can assure you that
if there's one man who has done more than anyone else to see
to it that MSS. and orchestral parts, from now on, must be
thoroughly disinfected before being submitted to him, that
man is our friend Lamoureux—and how right he is! Can you
see a chap whose rehearsals are going to cost him a nice little
sum of fourteen or fifteen hundred francs amusing himself by
correcting on the spot, while the orchestra waits, all the
mistakes the gentleman has left in? He doesn't waste any time,
I can tell you; I've even seen him practically hurl a score back
at a bloke s head, and after that there really was a clean-up, I
can assure you. In any case music today has become so prickly,
as Bloch would say, with sharps and flats and double-flats,
not to mention the *sf*, *pp* and all the rest, that it's in one's own
interest to mark them, as no one else will. But that's enough
on this subject—for have you noticed that when one embarks
on something one could, without fancying oneself as a writer
or man of letters, scribble at least 500 pages on the subject
quite as well as they could. After all, it's less complicated
than music . . .

In point of fact Chabrier had a better reason to fancy himself as a writer than most musicians; for it is quite evident from his letters that he had a definite literary gift, considerable powers of observation and the ability to record and express his impressions of people and things and the world about him. He was particularly sensitive to the beauties of nature, and a long letter he wrote to his wife towards the end of his life describing his impressions of places he was visiting in his native Auvergne has fortunately been preserved (Girardon). It is too long to quote in full, but the following extracts will give some idea of his perceptiveness and remarkable gift of creating a picture in words.

Mont-Dore, 15th August 1891.

. . . I want to tell you about the two excursions I've made, as for the last four or five days the weather has been marvellous, blue skies all the time and very hot. The country is AD-MIRABLE; it's less imposing than Cauterets [in the Pyrenees] where you can't move without bumping into a mountain at least 9,000 feet high which blocks your view, but it's sufficiently dramatic and above all, *delicious*. Mont-Dore itself is in a valley surrounded by high mountains which all have their own names, their legends, their pretty waterfalls, their Devil's Gorge etc., the tallest of which is the Pic du Sancy, visible from all sides, when it wants to be, and which can be climbed on foot in an afternoon—but it doesn't do to waste any time. But don't let's anticipate. The carriage went up and up, and suddenly I found myself looking at a wonderful panorama which seemed all the more beautiful because Mme Abry didn't say anything, wishing to observe my surprise. Yes, from the top of this hill, which must be some 4,500 feet above sea-level, I can see before my eyes two enormous rocks which appear to be slowly and insensibly climbing upwards, like gigantic pyramids, as if they were natural sentinels guarding an immense expanse of country, as far as the eye can see, studded with mounds and hills and rolling fields stretching

to the horizon like waves of many colours—violet, pink and
green, the whole landscape glowing red and gold and violet
under a burning sun. I have never seen anything so beautiful.
At six o'clock we returned to Mont-Dore. . . . But the best of
all was the excursion I made yesterday. After a long uphill
drive of some fifteen or sixteen kilometres, lasting four hours
and another hour to come down, we arrived at eleven a.m. at
the Château de Murols. I'll come back to that, but I must tell
you that the mountains the carriage had to keep going round
were continually changing in appearance so that the view was
never the same. At one moment we were trotting along at a
prodigious height; next we were dropping down again, zig-
zagging as the road descended steeply, winding its way
between waterfalls and gushing torrents and pinewoods that
seemed to be rushing past us—one felt bewildered, but I assure
you I've never seen anything more beautiful, and I was saying
all the time: If only my little one could be there! . . . Finally
we reached the castle, or rather the foot of the castle of
Murols; Murols is a charming little village on the edge of a
lake surrounded, of course, by mountains—because here all
the lakes are very high up—and this one was so calm you
could see to the bottom. Eventually we climbed up to the
château, which is absolutely in ruins, but extraordinarily
interesting; it dates from 1350, and belonged to two families,
the Murols and the d'Estaings. It took two centuries to build
—and the revolution of '89 ten minutes to destroy. . . . The
castle is of vast proportions, and the sight of its enormous,
battered skeleton still gives one a wonderful impression of
what it must have been like in feudal times, the scene of fierce
battles—you can see the holes in the walls through which the
defenders poured boiling oil and all kinds of horrors on to the
archers below—in a word, all the idiotic business you and I
must have seen in the historic pageants at the Porte Saint-
Martin when we were little. After tipping an old woman,
who looked medieval herself, and had acted as guide, we

scrambled down to Murols where the landau was waiting and
took the road back to Saint-Nectaire where we arrived soon
after noon, absolutely famished.

Then follows a description of the return journey to Mont-Dore:

To the tinkling of the bells on our two horses' collars we
climb into our carriage again and off we go—taking the same
road again and winding our way round the same enormous
mountains, the horses walking during the long uphill stretches
and trotting slowly on the long downhill gradients. Once
again we admired the marvellous panoramas of this beautiful
countryside, and soon we had to put our coats on because it was
now beginning to grow cooler; and with the cool air came the
exquisite scent of new-mown hay, and the scent seemed to
come from far away, as if from over the sea, strong and pene-
trating, as if we were being bathed in the *perspiration* of this
hot day—a most delicious sensation. Meanwhile on the slopes
of the mountains, as we passed them one after another, we
could see immense herds of cattle, nearly all the colour of
mahogany, winding their way down from the peaks, in straggl-
ing circles all the way to the bottom; and we could hear, as
if coming from very far away, first the sound of the cow-bells
tinkling out their mysterious little rhythms and then the
shepherds calling while their dogs ran madly about all over
these vast grass slopes flecked here and there with patches of a
deeper green—for by now night was falling; but we could see
the shepherds' little wooden carts, all painted white with
flowers round their wheels—the little carts which are pushed
by oxen and in which the shepherds, old and young alike,
sleep under the stars or in stormy weather, immutable and
unmoved, wrapped in their rough cloaks, never speaking and
looking—at what? At beautiful things, the lucky fellows.
And there they will sleep, the old shepherds and the boys,
for eight or ten days at a stretch before going home with their
enormous flocks. No *Echo de Paris* for them, but it's their

destiny to contemplate a spectacle that's continually renewed
by the march of time, and indeed when one has seen all these
beautiful things one can only envy people who, having no
preoccupations or problems of any kind, and knowing only
one way of living, invariably the same, are lucky to have such
things to look at; they're surely happy; they must be. *On the
other hand!!*—when winter comes and *everything* is covered with
snow forty to fifty feet deep it's impossible to do anything or
go anywhere; every house, every hut, every cottage, including
the shepherds' little carts—the whole place is sunk in a deep
sleep for six months—and woe to him who ventures out; he
could get lost within a few yards from his own doorstep, and
the long and dangerous roads are studded with crosses showing
where someone who lost his way died, smothered in a blizzard,
rolled like a cigarette and thrown far away; a little white hole
showing where he went in, more snow again to fill up the little
white hole—and it's all over. . . .

If it be true that a man's letters give us a deeper insight into his
true character than any other form of exteriorization of his
personality, then there is certainly much that we can learn from
the correspondence of Emmanuel Chabrier. He had the born
letter-writer's gift of spontaneous self-expression, with no undertones of insincerity or of writing for effect, combined with a
light touch, an ever-present sense of humour and a generous
measure of that facility which he so often complained he
lacked when writing music. He also found letters a convenient
form of making his views known on a variety of subjects, especially music and musicians, in a way that, not being a professional
writer or critic, was the only one open to him. One last quotation
now from a letter (the addressee is unspecified) showing Chabrier
as a critic of the musical scene around him in the year 1889.[7]
Armand Silvestre (1837–1901), to whom he had evidently been
writing with reference to some text he was proposing to set, was
a minor poet to whom many nineteenth-century French composers,

Another example of Chambrier's originality as a correspondent

notably Fauré, de Castillon and Duparc, turned for librettos and verses to set as songs. Evidently not all that he wrote found favour in Chabrier's eyes:

I wrote today to Silvestre and explained to him what I want. What I don't want, for example, are those external flower-beds in three couplets where people idiotically go to pick chrysanthemums or begonias; what I don't want are those banalities about love in springtime, especially April or May; let's give those two months of the year a rest—they've been overworked as much as the little flowers in the garden. After all, didn't some bloke once say: Why not leave the roses to the rose tree? I couldn't agree more. And, unless I'm much mistaken, Armand must have turned out something like 300,000 sonnets and bits and pieces on these themes—as you and Lacome and Baudon know only too well. And Lacome does it very well. Since then, and always about April and May and the flowers of the fields and other nonsense of this kind, young Bordes, Chausson, Marty, Bréville, Hüe, Debussy & Co. have all composed ingenious and *recherché* songs, but with such tormented, and often sad, tearful and despairing music that when they're sung in drawing-rooms you feel as if the singer is either burying the devil or bringing the Last Sacraments to the audience.[8] As soon as the lady opens her mouth, I say to myself: That's right, my dear; carry on; you're going to wring my withers again with a 'De profundis ad te clamavi, Domine'! All I can say is I'm fed up to the ears with all this; I can't see anyone except Fauré and Holmès who can get away from all this sob-stuff.[9] I want to write something *gay*; I mean gay for *both sexes*; something robust and simple—fables or stories—at any rate something different from Fauré and Holmès and all the rest of them. Silvestre and Richepin are excellent for that sort of thing, but not Catulle; useless to suggest it to him. It's *difficult*, since out of every ten persons who lean against a piano and appear to give pleasure to their audience, eight at least are women; so you've got to remember that and try to do something that will please them. It's obvious that Mme Carou, for example, couldn't sing 'Le petit vin Rousillon' in *Une Education manquée* and do the tongue-smacking in which Lecointe was without a rival. So what I'm asking won't be easy. Think about it and tell me whether you think my idea is a good one. . . . The first act of *Briséis* is not nearly finished, far from it. Since I left I've been held up by a certain situation; I haven't been able to hit on anything that satisfies me, and I haven't kept anything that I've written these

last few days. It's excessively difficult; and for me what makes
it all the more difficult is that I'm absolutely determined not
to be *boring*—and upon my word there are places where it
would seem that that's just what is required!!! I know exactly
what I mean by that—anyone in our profession would understand me perfectly. But I don't want that, and that makes it
terribly difficult. Moreover (just as it was with *Gwendoline*
which, if you remember, was begun in July 1879) it will be
impossible for me to write these acts immediately one after
the other; I should repeat myself; my ideas wouldn't have
the same freshness or variety that I could count on if I allowed
my work to rest for a while. In the meantime I shall do something else. But when? I don't know; but above all it's no good
writing platitudes. Massenet is writing *Esclarmonde* in six
months; Reyer's taking ten years to fabricate *Salammbô*;
everyone does what he can. As I never stop telling myself, if
I were as gifted as old father Bach things would be a lot better.

The reader has by now had an opportunity of judging Chabrier's
prowess as a letter-writer. Who then were the correspondents to
whom the majority of his letters were addressed? Apart from his
wife and family and the faithful Nanine, they were either great
personal friends like the tenor van Dyck, the composers Charles
Lecocq, Vincent d'Indy, Paul Lacome d'Estalenx and Edouard
Moullé (*see* Note 2, Chapter Three, page 157) or those with whom
he had business as well as friendly relations such as his publishers
M. and Mme Enoch and their partner Costallat, his librettist
Catulle Mendès and the impresario Henri Verdhurt, and last but
not least the conductor Felix Mottl, who was responsible for
making his music known in Germany.

The circle of his friends in the musical and literary world with
whom he did not necessarily carry on a regular correspondence
was of course much wider, and one of his closest friends and
boon companions was the Belgian critic and translator of Wagner's
operas, Victor Wilder (1835–92) who, like Chabrier, was closely

associated with Lamoureux in his campaign to introduce
Wagner's works to France in the 1880s. Less of a Bohemian and
more of a scholar than Wilder was the critic and aesthete Jules de
Brayer, who had been called, in a study devoted to him in *Le
Temps* (1929) by Louis Schneider, 'Chabrier's second conscience'.
De Brayer was one of the earliest champions of Mussorgsky's
music in France and a friend of Debussy. He had been the organist
of Chartres Cathedral, and had transcribed for the organ some
parts of *Boris Godunov* which he played on the Trocadero organ
at the close of the 1878 Exhibition in Paris. Strangely enough,
it would seem that this was actually the first performance in
France of any work by Mussorgsky. De Brayer had also collaborated with Lamoureux in the administration of his concerts, and
it is probable that his friendship with Chabrier dated from this
period.

  Many of the musicians of the Franckist school were his friends,
notably Duparc, de Bréville, Chausson and Charles Bordes; while
for 'Le Père Franck' himself Chabrier had the greatest admiration
and respect, although he never came under his influence in any
way. Nevertheless he was on the best of terms with the older
man, and in the circumstances it was not surprising that d'Indy
asked Chabrier to deputize for him at the graveside and deliver
the farewell speech at Franck's funeral. (*See* Chapter Seven.)

  What is really surprising, in view of what we know of Vincent
d'Indy's character and ideals, is the warm and indubitably sincere
friendship he felt for Chabrier, whose genius he was one of the
first to recognize after the production of *L'Etoile* had revealed a
new star in the Parisian musical firmament. The two men were,
one would have thought, fundamentally opposed in character;
on the one side the aristocratic Vicomte, a strict Catholic and
patriot, moralist and doctrinaire, whose whole approach to music
was more that of an academician and theorist than of an instinctive and spontaneous artist; on the other, the little man from the
Auvergne, bubbling over with high spirits and exuding music
from every pore, uninhibited in speech and manners, always

ready for a joke and the sworn enemy of conventions and taboos
in life and art alike. Don Quixote and Sancho Panza, in fact; a
musical knight errant and his faithful squire. Even physically,
the parallel holds good. It is all to d'Indy's credit that he realized
what a fine musician Chabrier was; and it is evidence of Chabrier's
catholicity of taste that he was able to see in d'Indy's music, so
different from his own, qualities that he was able to admire
unreservedly. It must be remembered that d'Indy was ten years
his junior, and had Chabrier lived on into the twentieth century
he might not perhaps have felt the same admiration for some of
his later works. There was, of course, a shared enthusiasm for
Wagner, which was one of the reasons that brought them together;
but perhaps more important still was the fact that both men,
despite their admiration for the German master, were basically
and essentially Frenchmen at heart and determined to keep their
own music free from any foreign influence. And it can be said
without hesitation that so far as the *best* works of both composers
are concerned they succeeded in doing just that.

It is to be regretted that we have no record of any significant
encounters between Chabrier and Debussy, although we have
seen that Chabrier had the rare distinction of being almost the
only contemporary French composer whom Debussy genuinely
admired; Lalo was the other. Of Chabrier's views on Debussy
however, we know next to nothing, although in the last years of
his life he would have been able to hear at least the String Quartet,
L'Après-midi d'un faune, several of the early songs, including the
first series of *Fêtes galantes*, and one or two of the early piano
pieces. There is no reason to suppose that he would have found
these works too 'advanced', because he was in sympathy with the
new music, admired Berlioz and Wagner and, among his contemporaries, Bizet, who at that time was looked upon as very
advanced, if not revolutionary.[10] The inclusion of Debussy in
the company of Bordes, Chausson, de Bréville and others accused
in the letter quoted above, of writing exclusively gloomy and
depressing songs seems, in any case, singularly inapt; but perhaps

Chabrier was thinking only of songs like *Il pleure dans mon cœur* or *Spleen*, ignoring things like *Fantoches* or *Mandoline* which could hardly be described as funereal.

It would also be interesting to know what he thought of Satie's music; and here again it is disappointing that there is no record of their having met, although we do know that, like Debussy, Satie approved of Chabrier, bracketing him in one of his tirades against academicism in music with Debussy and Dukas.[11] (Similarly, Ravel bracketed Chabrier with Satie as the two French composers who seemed to him to be the most 'necessary'.) Satie would certainly have relished the *Pastorale des petits cochons roses* and the *Ballade des gros dindons*; the ironic sentimentality of the *Petits cochons* and the solemn drollery of the *Gros dindons* have a definitely Satie-an flavour which puts them in very much the same category as, say, the *Descriptions automatiques* or *Avant-dernières pensées* of the 'Bon Maître'. We have seen how both men began experimenting at almost the same time with the 'new' harmonies which were later to become the everyday language of Debussy and Ravel (e.g. sequences of unrelated and unresolved chords of the ninth) and how both were imbued with the spirit of nonconformity. It would, however, be a mistake to exaggerate the points they had in common, Chabrier for all his boisterous exuberance being at heart a romantic inclined to lyrical effusiveness and capable of dealing with the larger forms of music, whereas Satie worked on a smaller scale in a restricted field of his own invention, quizzically questioning established values and acting generally as a kind of Socratic gad-fly.

Another contemporary artist who must, one would have thought, had some contact with Chabrier (although disappointingly there seems to be no direct evidence that this was the case) was Alfred Jarry, the irrepressible author of *Ubu Roi*. Nevertheless Professor Shattuck (1959) has suggested that

one obvious and neglected source of the action of *Ubu Roi* is the libretto of Chabrier's comic opera *Le Roi malgré lui* which

concerns a fictitious King of Poland, Laski, his *grand palatin*
(out of which title Jarry & Co. forged the three *palotins* or
'palatoons') and a generally farcical sequence of events. The
opera had its widely discussed *première* in 1887, just the year
before Jarry entered the *Lycée* in Rennes. . . .

Perhaps one reason why it is impossible to establish any closer
connection between Chabrier and such extreme, not to say
eccentric, nonconformists as Satie and Jarry is that Chabrier's
'bohemianism' was tempered to some extent by his associations
with certain more orthodox sections of Parisian society—Catulle
Mendès and his circle, for example—especially those connected with
the theatre, whose influence on the composer was deplored by many
of his friends. Mendès, who was by birth a Portuguese Jew, was
a prominent member of the Parnassian group of poets and an
industrious if somewhat superficial purveyor of not only poetry,
but plays and novels which he produced in large numbers. He
also specialized, as a profitable sideline, in providing librettos
for operatically inclined composers, of whom Chabrier was one
of his most faithful clients. He was married for a time to Théophile Gautier's daughter Judith, who moved in musical circles
and had at one time an *affaire* with Wagner; while he himself had
a liaison for some years with the Franco-Irish composer Augusta
Holmès by whom he had three daughters, one of whom sub-
sequently married Henri Barbusse, author of *Le Feu*, a contro-
versial left-wing novel based on the author's experiences in the
1914 war.

Apart from Mendès, however, Chabrier had many other literary
contacts. Indeed, in reviewing his life and work as a whole, what
seems to single him out from most other composers of his time
is the ease with which he seems to have penetrated all the different
milieux, literary and artistic as well as musical, and to have won
the respect and friendship of painters and men of letters as well
as of his fellow musicians. He collaborated with Verlaine, gave
composition lessons to Villiers de l'Isle-Adam, set to music

verses by Edmond Rostand (author of *Chantecler* and *Cyrano de Bergerac*) and Jean Richepin, the poet of the underworld of tramps and vagrants; and he frequented the literary *salons*, notably that of the famous Nina de Callias, who played hostess to all the literary and artistic *élite* of Paris in the 1880s, where he would have rubbed shoulders with, among others, the Goncourt brothers, Huysmans, Zola, Alphonse Daudet and Mallarmé. But it was above all the keen interest he took in painting and his associations with the Impressionists that distinguished Chabrier from the majority of his contemporaries in the musical world; and it is that aspect of him we have now to consider in greater detail, with special reference to the remarkable collection of pictures he acquired during his lifetime of which a brief account will be given in the chapter that follows.

CHAPTER TEN

Chabrier and the Impressionists—The Musician and his painter friends—Collector and connoisseur.

THE CONNECTION between the plastic arts and music has not always been recognized as openly and universally as it is today. Indeed, it could be said that it was not until the twentieth century that the tendency to stress not so much the differences that separate the arts as the features and qualities they have in common become apparent; and today such a view is widely accepted. Without going all the way with Skryabin (1872–1915), who dreamed of uniting all the arts together in a vast symposium in which sounds and colours, words and plastic designs and even scents would be blended in one great apocalyptic 'Mystery' in which all the senses would be simultaneously engaged, modern aestheticians are moving in the same direction. Composers give visual titles to their music; painters evoke sounds and devise counterpoints for the eye and poets likewise appeal simultaneously to the eye and ear with visual images and evocative sonorities. This new tendency to 'fuse' the arts could be said to have started in the last decades of the nineteenth century. The Impressionist painters were concerned to create an 'atmosphere' rather than, like those of the realist school, to portray the 'thing itself'. The difference between the two techniques is like the generic difference between painting and photography: the one is essentially a reconstruction (subjective), the other an imitation (objective). Nevertheless, paradoxically enough, Impressionism in painting owed its origin to a desire for greater scientific precision, and the first Impressionists were concerned above all to bring their painting into line with certain definite scientific laws relating to light and the refraction of the sun's rays.

This impressionistic style (the word 'impressionist' was at first applied to the pioneer painters of that school in a derogatory sense) gradually came to be accepted and, by a natural transition, soon began to have an influence upon music. It only remained to translate the impressionist theory from terms of light to terms of sound, and for musicians to proceed to put it into practice. Blurred outlines were soon found to be just as feasible in music as in painting, and the scintillating effects of sunlight found their counterpart in shimmering harmonies and the skilfully blended vibrations of 'upper partials'. Just as the painters 'decomposed' a ray of light, so did musicians split up the 'fundamental' (harmonic root) into its numerous sonorous component parts, thereby creating the kind of harmonies which Debussy was to make so characteristically his own. But even before Debussy there had been Erik Satie (notably in his *Sarabandes* published in 1887) and there had also been Emmanuel Chabrier who, with Satie, was one of the first to write progressions of unrelated and unresolved chords of the seventh and ninth, as we saw in, for example, the opening bars of *Le Roi malgré lui* (*see* page 72).

But there is no doubt that Satie was one of the first musicians to establish a definite link between music and painting when he suggested to Debussy, when the latter was contemplating making an opera out of Maeterlinck's *Pelléas et Mélisande*: 'What we have to do is to create a musical scenery, a musical atmosphere in which the characters move and talk—a certain atmosphere that suggests Puvis de Chavannes.' [1] And in a lecture on Debussy which Satie gave much later he had this to say:

Debussy's aesthetic is symbolist in some of his works and impressionist in most. Please forgive me, for am not I a little bit responsible? . . . At that time I was writing music for *Le Fils des Etoiles* on a text by Joseph Péladan, and I explained to Debussy the necessity for a Frenchman to free himself from the Wagnerian adventure, which in no way corresponded to our national aspirations. And I told him that I was not anti-Wagner in any way, but that we ought to have our own music —if possible without *choucroute*. Why shouldn't we make

use of the methods employed by Claude Monet, Cézanne,
Toulouse-Lautrec, etc. etc. . . ? Nothing simpler. Aren't they
just expressions? That would have been the origin of a new
start which would have led to results which would be almost
bound to be successful. . . .

And, although Debussy repudiated the label 'impressionist',
much of his music has visual associations, and his interest in
painting ranged from the Pre-Raphaelites in his youth to Turner
and Hokusai in later life, as well as to painters like Puvis de
Chavannes, Whistler and the so-called Neo-Impressionists who
flourished during the years of his maturity.

The object of this digression, as will now be seen, is to make
the point that, although the connection between music and
painting was firmly established by the beginning of the twentieth
century, the musicians who were interested enough in painting
in the 1880s not only to buy contemporary works, but even to
think of applying to music some of the newest pictorial techniques, were indeed few and far between. All the more surprising,
then, that one of the pioneers in this field should have been the
self-taught musician from the Auvergne who, within a few
years of his arrival in the capital, had developed a quite extraordinary flair for all that was most significant in the work of the
young *avant-garde* painters of the day. As if by instinct he was
drawn towards the 'Impressionists', who at that time were being
publicly reviled and treated rather as if they were criminal
lunatics. Not only did he make friends with them, but he
actually bought their works; moreover, there is no doubt that,
consciously or unconsciously, Chabrier tended in his music to
introduce effects which owe more than a little to impressionist
techniques in the handling of colour and light. This is apparent
no less in many of the keyboard works than in the larger orchestral
frescoes, such as *España* or *Joyeuse Marche*, where timbres are mixed
and contrasted like pigments on the painter's palette; while some
of the piano pieces, notably *Idylle* and *Sous-bois* and the *Bourrée*,

are so atmospheric that in the former one can almost *feel* the contrast between sun and shade, while in the latter the colour is laid on so thick that the ear is dazzled as the eye would be if the impression were purely visual.

Among the famous painters whose pictures Chabrier bought at a time when they were not so much famous as notorious, were Manet, Monet, Forain and Renoir; while with Manet especially he struck up a friendship which lasted until the latter's death. At the sale of Manet's paintings in 1884 Chabrier was able (thanks to a legacy which his wife had received) to buy, at prices which today seem ridiculous, several important works, including the celebrated *Bar aux Folies-Bergère*, which for the last ten years of his life hung over the piano in his studio in the Avenue Trudaine. Some idea of the richness and variety of Chabrier's collection of pictures can be gained from the following catalogue issued in connection with the public auction at which these works were offered for sale after the composer's death.

CATALOGUE
de
TABLEAUX
Pastels
Aquarelles, Dessins
Eaux-Fortes et Lithographies
composant la collection
EMMANUEL CHABRIER
et dont la vente aura lieu
Hôtel Drouot, Salle No. 6
Le Jeudi, 26 Mars 1896
à trois heures

Commissaire-Priseur
Me. Paul Chavellier
10, rue Grange-Batelière (10e.)

Expert
M. Durand-Ruel
16, Rue Laffitte (16e.)

EXPOSITION
Le mercredi 25 mars 1896, de 1h.$\frac{1}{2}$ à 5h.$\frac{1}{2}$

The following is a list, with the prices realized (when known) of the principal works, omitting a few by minor artists such as Cazin (Jean-Charles, 1841–1901), Clairin (Georges-Jules-Victor, 1843–1920), Flameng (Marie-Auguste, 1843–93), Jacquet (Gustave-Jean, 1846–?) and Meunier (Constantin, 1831–1905).[2]

I. OIL PAINTINGS

Arist	Title	Price (Francs)
Cézanne	Les Moissonneurs	500
Helleu	La Femme à l'ombrelle	
Manet	Un Bar aux Folies-Bergère	Withdrawn Reserve: 23,000
,,	Le Skating	Withdrawn Reserve: 10,000
,,	Vase de fleurs	1,100
,,	Jeune fille dans les fleurs	450
,,	Le Lièvre	1,000
,,	Bateaux de pêche	900
,,	Au café (sketch)	705
Monet	Les Bords de la Seine	2,600
,,	Effets de neige	1,500
,,	La Maison de campagne	1,100
,,	Le Parc Monceau	3,050
,,	Les Bords de la Seine	3,600
,,	La Fête nationale, rue du Faubourg-Saint-Denis	2,200
Renoir	La Sortie du Conservatoire	1,500
,,	Femme nue	8,000
,,	Femme faisant du crochet	650
Sisley	Canotiers à Hampton Court	980
,,	La Seine au Point-du-Jour	1,850

II. Pastels, Water-colours and Drawings

Artist	Title	Price (Francs)
Forain	*Etude de femme*	
Helleu	*Buste de femme*	
Manet (drawing)	*Au théâtre: le Paradis*	95
Monet (pastel)	*Gamins et gamines*	200
,, (pastel)	*Coucher de soleil*	95
Renoir (pastel)	*Jeune femme au chapeau de paille*	410
,, (pastel)	*Le Repos*	1,000
,, (pastel)	*Buste de femme*	355

III. Etchings and Lithographs

Forain	*Le Bouquet*	
Manet (etching, after Velasquez)	*Seigneurs espagnols*	80
Manet (lithograph)	*Les Courses*	35
Manet (lithograph)	*Episode de la Commune*	45

For the light which it throws on Chabrier's remarkable universality of mind and sensitivity to and appreciation of all forms of artistic expression I have thought it worth while to quote the following warm appreciation of the man in the Introduction to the catalogue of the sale of these pictures (now part of the Don Chabrier Collection in the Bibliothèque Nationale) written by André Maurel, art critic of *Le Figaro* and son-in-law of Chabrier's great friend Victor Wilder.

This collection is certainly not that of an amateur. Nor is it that of a painter. It is something better still—the collection of an artist. And by that I mean of a man with a taste for Beauty, responsive to every manifestation of all kinds of temperaments in every artistic domain—a man who was not only the brilliant composer of *Gwendoline* but the friend of Paul Verlaine and Manet.

Such universal temperaments are rare—and one can be sure that they are the external sign of an exceptional intelligence. What, then, are we to think when, as in Chabrier's case, this wide understanding is allied to such an intense and highly strung sensibility and to such continuous mental activity? It was this perpetual cerebral agitation that caused the death of our poor friend. *He died from being unable to live without enthusiasm.* When he rose from his work table, it was not rest that he was seeking, but, in looking at his pictures, emotions of another kind, no less lively and exhausting. From *Gwendoline* to Renoir's *Femme nue*, from *España* to his Manets, he went with exuberant delight revelling, in a way I have never seen before, in pure beauty. There is no need to describe the pictures of which Emmanuel Chabrier's little collection is composed. You have only to look through this catalogue to see that every picture marks a stage in the life of the artist who painted it. Each one is a date in the history of art, from the early Monets down to the *Bar aux Folies-Bergère*.

For ourselves, what each of these pictures represents is a date in the life of our friend. With each one we associate an event in his life, a manifestation of that burning enthusiasm that enabled him to discern in the early works of Monet the great artist that was to be, and thus to be almost the first to understand the intensely poetic nature of this great painter.

Moreover all the artists in this catalogue were his friends. With Manet his association could not have been closer or more devoted. Manet died in his arms. And shortly before he died, Chabrier expressed his wish to be buried at Passy along with the two friends he loved best in the world, Victor Wilder and Manet.

And so, to see Chabrier's pictures being dispersed is like seeing the familiar belongings of people one loves being thrown out of the window. It's not only pictures that all you faithful and discerning amateurs will be buying; it's a part of the very inmost soul and spirit of the great composer of *Gwendoline* and *Briséis*; and every time I look at them—alas! tomorrow I shall not be able to do this any more—between them and me I feel the presence of my friend, and it seems as if the warm and tender affection he had lavished on them were being radiated by the pictures themselves. You amateurs who are going to possess them now, I beg of you to care for them devotedly. For they are not only master-works but—and it is this that makes them twice as precious—pictures that have been chosen and loved by a great artist.

The fact that this great artist was himself a musician renders this tribute all the more moving and unusual. It also makes it in a sense unique, for it is not easy to think of any other famous composer to whom it could have been addressed. There have been others, of course, who have shown in varying degrees an interest in the plastic arts—Debussy, for example, in modern times—or have even, like Schönberg or Messiaen (who has confessed to having done some scene-painting in his youth), been painters themselves; but such cases are very rare.

Of the portraits of Chabrier painted by Manet and others it is perhaps unfortunate that the brilliantly clever but somewhat overcharged caricature of the composer, apparently demolishing a piano, by his friend Edouard Detaille should be the best known —at least to the general public—since it has helped to create the impression that Chabrier was a kind of musical clown. It has been my object in these pages, while not attempting to deny or minimize the delightful earthiness and Rabelaisian coarseness of one side of his complex character, occasionally reflected in his music, to dispel the image conveyed in Detaille's caricature—or rather, to make it clear that this aspect of his personality was only one of many. In reality Chabrier's life was in some respect a tragic one. During barely fifteen years of creative activity he suffered the disappointment of not obtaining in his own country the full recognition he felt he was entitled to; while the last years of his life were clouded by the terrible paralysis which prevented him from achieving fully what he felt he had been put into this world to achieve, and induced in him that mental distress which found expression in the pathetic words of disillusionment, already quoted, addressed to the beloved art to whose service his life had been devoted: 'Pauvre chère musique, pauvre chère amie—tu ne veux donc plus que je sois heureux!' Manet's portrait (Plate 6), shown here, has captured most convincingly the dreamy, contemplative side of the composer of the *Ode à la Musique*, but, when all is said and done, the best portrait of the man who, in Poulenc's words, 'a fait entrer la tendresse et la joie dans la musique française', is the portrait he painted of himself—in his music.

NOTES

CHAPTER ONE

1. The title 'Parnassian' was adopted by a group of young poets in revolt against the old Romantic school represented by Victor Hugo, Lamartine and their contemporaries, and symbolized their spiritual affinities with the Latin and Hellenic tradition of the old sixteenth-century poets of the Pléiade, headed by Ronsard and du Bellay, and also with the new school represented by Théodore de Banville (1823–91), Théophile Gautier (1811–72) and Charles Baudelaire (1821–67). A precision of language and technical perfection which did not exclude an extreme sensibility, though expressed with detachment, was their ideal; and in some ways they could be considered the forerunners of the 'art for art's sake' movement which flourished at the end of the century. With the help of the *avant-garde* publisher Alphonse Lemerre they launched, on 2nd March 1866, the first number of their Review, *Le Parnasse contemporain*. Prominent members of the Parnassian group were François Coppée (1842–1908), Sully Prudhomme (1839–1907), Stéphane Mallarmé (1842–98) and Paul Verlaine (1844–96). Catulle Mendès (1841–1909) was an indifferent and very prolific *littérateur* who wrote, among other things, librettos for a number of composers and was closely associated with Chabrier (upon whom he was considered by many to have had a bad influence), who commissioned him to write the librettos of his two most important operas, *Gwendoline* and the unfinished *Briséis*.

2. *Fisch-ton-Khan*: presumably a humorous distortion of the vulgar French slang expression *ficher le camp*, meaning 'hop it', or 'skedaddle'.

3. The fragments constituting the first of these little works are described as: 'Cinq numéros d'une operette intitulée Fisch-ton-Kan, paroles de Paul Verlaine.' Four are scored for voice and

155

piano; the last (a trio) for orchestra alone. The titles are:

(1) *Petit morceau de scène* (entrée du pitre) [clown's entry].

(2) *Couplets de Poussah* ('J'engraisse, mon front brille d'allegresse').

(3) *Air et duo* (Fisch, puis Soulgouly).

(4) *Petit ensemble* ('Il faut bien avoir de l'humanité').

(5) *Trio* (Soulgouly, Fisch-ton-Khan, Kakao).

The second set of sketches (both are written in pencil, as was Chabrier's custom) is inscribed: 'Musique composée pour une opérette *Vaucochard et Fils Ier*, paroles de Verlaine, en 1864 (*partition orchestre et chant*).' There are four numbers:

(1) *Chanson de l'homme armé.*

(2) *Duo* (Aglaé et Médéric).

(3) *Sérénade.*

(4) *Trio* (Aglaé, Vaucochard, Médéric).

The autograph MS. of these pieces is in the collection of M. André Meyer, by whose kind permission the titles and inscriptions are reproduced here.

4. The writer, Lucien Viotti, who had been Verlaine's schoolmate at the Lycée Bonaparte. He was killed during the Franco-Prussian war in 1870.

CHAPTER TWO

1. Except where otherwise stated all quotations throughout this book from Chabrier's letters are taken from Joseph Desaymard's *Chabrier d'après ses lettres*.

2. The fact that Vincent d'Indy shortly afterwards wrote a symphony on the theme of Hunyadi Janos suggests that he may have been prompted by Chabrier to do so. This symphony, though never published, was performed in Paris at a Société Nationale concert in 1875 (incomplete) and again, after completion, in 1876.

CHAPTER THREE

1. Henri Duparc (1848–1933). Favourite pupil of César Franck, the composer of some immortal songs as fine as any in the modern French repertory, the best known being: *L'Invitation au voyage* (Baudelaire); *Phydilé* (Leconte de Lisle); *Chanson triste* (Jean Lahor); *Lamento* (Théophile Gautier); *Extase* (Lahor); *La Vie antérieure* (Baudelaire). Despite his immense talent, Duparc ceased composing at the age of thirty-eight, though he lived to be eighty-five, having been afflicted with a mysterious neuro-psychic malady which paralysed his creative faculties.

2. Edouard Manet (1832–83), leader of French Impressionists; Ernest Chausson (1855–99), Franck pupil and friend of Debussy; Vincent d'Indy (1851–1931) most eminent composer of Franckist school, Director of the *Schola Cantorum* in Paris; Pierre de Bréville (1861–1949), composer and teacher at the *Schola*; André Messager (1853–1929) light opera composer (*Véronique*, etc.) and conductor; directed first performances of *Pelléas et Mélisande*. Camille Saint-Saëns (1835–1921), key figure in nineteenth-century French music; Charles Lecocq (1832–1918) light opera composer (*La Fille de Madame Angot, Giroflé-Girofla*, etc.); Paul Lacome d'Estalenx (1838–1921) light opera composer (*Jeanne, Jeannette et Jeanneton, La Gardeuse d'oies*, etc.) great personal friend of Chabrier, as was Edouard Moullé (1845–?). 'Le Père Moullé', who had a famous piano shop in the rue Blanche, collected and edited folk songs from Normandy and Spain.

CHAPTER FOUR

1. Chabrier was wrong; Enoch & Costallat lost no time in publishing the *Trois Valses*, which came out in 1883.

2. From a lecture delivered by Vincent d'Indy on Chabrier and Dukas at a Pasdeloup historical concert on 8th April 1920. (*Bibliothèque Nationale*.)

CHAPTER FIVE

1. In a lecture delivered on 4th April 1920 at a memorial concert for Chabrier and Paul Dukas.

2. François-Auguste Gevaert (1828–1908), the distinguished Belgian musicologist and Director of the Brussels Conservatoire from 1871 to 1908.

3. Mottl was one of the great Wagnerian conductors appearing frequently at Bayreuth together with Hans Richter (1843–1916) and Hermann Levi (1839–1900).

4. *Gwendoline* was revived and performed again at the Opéra (apparently for the last time) in 1911, and enthusiastically reviewed in the international press. Thus the critic of the *Tribune de Genève* (17th March 1911) praised especially the 'admirable architecture . . . sonority and plenitude . . . of the *Epithalamium*' which he described as 'remarkable from every point of view', while the opera as a whole he pronounced to be 'of great musical value, and belonging to no school. . . .'

Le Journal de Genève, for its part (18th March 1911), described Chabrier as 'a master, one of the most original composers of the whole mid nineteenth-century French school', and dealt with the question of Chabrier's alleged indebtedness to Wagner as follows: '. . . The orchestra is treated with superb mastery, in the Wagnerian sense and according to the methods of the master of Bayreuth . . . but it is in the orchestra alone that this influence is noticeable, because the work still preserves the old-fashioned operatic formula of arias, duets and *ensemble* numbers. . . .'

In *Le Petit Havre* of 2nd April 1911 Henri Woollett, the Franco-British musicologist, wrote an enthusiastic appreciation of Chabrier on the occasion of this revival of his opera, hailing him as the precursor of the modern school of French music: 'Chabrier is a profoundly original composer; his music resembles nothing but himself. He has discovered melodic and expressive formulae of a very special kind. His harmonization, extremely bold but

with a flavour and elegance all its own, already foreshadows all
the discoveries of the younger school and has not been without
influence on all our most modern composers. And yet his delicate
and refined art is above all remarkable for its spontaneity, clarity
and expressive power which certainly are the result of inspiration
rather than reflection. . . .'

CHAPTER SIX

1. In the published edition this appears to have been omitted.

2. Brussel, who died in 1940, had collected the unpublished
correspondence between Chabrier and Mottl which after his
death was passed by his widow to M. Roger Delage with permission to publish. The letters eventually appeared in *La Revue
de Musicologie*, vol. xlix, in July 1963, and it is to this invaluable
source that I am indebted for all quotations from this fascinating
correspondence, and also from the letters exchanged between
Mottl and Cosima Wagner. My translations are from the French
of M. Delage, who has translated Mottl's original German
(which he also prints).

3. Mottl was one of the first to play Berlioz in Germany, and
gave the first complete performance of *Les Troyens* in Carlsruhe
in 1890.

4. Richter was chief conductor of the Vienna Opera and Phil-
harmonic Orchestra, and Wilhelm Jahn (1839–1900) was from
1881 to 1897 Director of the Vienna Opera.

CHAPTER SEVEN

1. It appears that the piece was written as a sight-reading test
for junior pupils at the Bordeaux Conservatoire, but was so
difficult that it was pronounced unplayable—even for four hands
let alone two. Chabrier pretended to be astonished at this finding;
but it is possible the piece was intended as a 'leg-pull'—to scare
the Director and tease the students.

2. It is regrettable that such an apparently interesting work should be out of circulation. The unpublished MS., once in the possession of Robert Brussel's widow, cannot now be traced.

3. In point of fact, neither *Gwendoline* nor *Le Roi* was ever produced in Vienna, although at one time Chabrier thought that Richter was definitely interested in *Le Roi* and had in fact told him that he thought it would have a great success in Vienna because 'our composers do not write *opéras-comiques* with lively, gay, exciting rhythms; they either write pseudo-Wagner or cheap operettas. . . .' But Richter apparently lost interest, and the project came to nothing.

4. Almost certainly he is referring to *Lucia di Lammermoor* by Donizetti (1797–1848).

5. Paul Vidal (1863–1931), composer, conductor and teacher, founder of the *Concerts de l'Opéra*. As a winner of the *Grand Prix de Rome* he was with Debussy at the Villa Medicis in Rome, and it is on record that when Liszt visited the Villa in 1885 Vidal and Debussy played for him Chabrier's *Trois valses romantiques* for two pianos.

CHAPTER EIGHT

1. If this is music that 'charms', we should recall Jean Cocteau's aphorism on this subject: 'Charm demands perfect tact. It means standing on the brink of an abyss. Nearly all the "graceful" artists fall into it. Rossini, Tchaikovsky, Weber, Gounod, Chabrier and, today, Francis Poulenc lean over but do not fall. A very deep root enables them to lean a very long way.' *Le Rappel à l'Ordre* (appendix to *Cock and Harlequin*), 1926.

2. The text of the letter, dated 1st March 1893, from Bertrand, the Director of the Paris Opéra, announcing his decision to mount *Gwendoline* (for facsimile see Plate 7), was as follows: 'I am happy to bring you good news which I hope will hasten your recovery.

Gwendoline, your fine work which Paris ought to have heard long ago, will be produced this year at the Opéra. Get well quickly so that you can come yourself to supervise rehearsals. . . .'

CHAPTER NINE

1. This does not mean that his standards were not invariably high. For rubbishy music, of the kind which he characteristically described as 'musique que ce n'est pas la peine', he had nothing but contempt.

2. *Excelsior,* an 'historical apotheosis of human civilization', was a *Ballet à grand spectacle* by Romualdo Marenco of La Scala of Milan, produced at the Eden Theatre in Paris in 1889 where it had tremendous success; *Jean Chevalier,* an opera by Victorin de Joncières (1839–1903); *Fra Diavolo,* by Auber (1782–1871); *Belisario* by Donizetti (1794–1848); *Mireille* and *Philémon et Baucis* by Gounod (1818–93).

3. *Lohengrin* first performed in Paris by Lamoureux when Chabrier was his assistant. (*See* Chapter Three.)

4. From a lecture delivered by d'Indy on 8th April 1920 at one of the Pasdeloup historical concerts devoted to the music of Chabrier and Duparc. Original in the *Bibliothèque Nationale.*

5. His beautiful and unusual handwriting is especially noticeable and should interest graphologists.

6. The books in question were: *Mes hôpitaux* (in prose) and *Chansons pour Elle* by Verlaine; *Episodes* by Henri de Regnier; *A travers un vitrail* by Willete; *Le Dernier Album* (an album of verse and drawings) by André Gill.

7. I am able to quote from this unpublished autograph letter by kind permission of M. Marc Pincherle.

8. Charles Bordes (1863–1909), a pupil of César Franck and one of the founders of the *Schola Cantorum* in 1894; Ernest Chausson (1855–99), a pupil of Franck, composer of talent and friend and

benefactor of Debussy; Georges Marty (1860–1908), conductor and composer, a pupil of Massenet; Pierre de Bréville (1861–1949), a pupil of Franck, composer of distinction; Georges Hue (1858–1948) *Prix de Rome*, wrote operas, e.g. *Les Pantins* produced at the Opéra-Comique in 1881; Debussy (1862–1918).

9. This was Augusta Holmès (1847–1903), the Franco-Irish composer who was a great celebrity in her day in Parisian musical and literary circles. (See *Augusta Holmès: a meteoric career*, by Rollo Myers in *The Musical Quarterly*, July 1967.)

10. It is perhaps not generally known that the full score open on the piano at which Chabrier is seated in Fantin-Latour's picture *Autour du Piano* is that of *Carmen*, placed there at the suggestion of d'Indy and Chabrier as a mark of respect and admiration for its composer.

11. Professor Roger Shattuck records that 'after hearing *Le Roi malgré lui* Satie sent Chabrier one of his own magnificently copied and inscribed compositions (in red ink and Gothic script). There was no reply'. (One cannot but wonder why.)

CHAPTER TEN

1. Puvis de Chavannes (1824–98) painted classical and semi-classical subjects in a decorative style of which the best known examples, perhaps, are the murals in his characteristic pale, rather faded colours in the Panthéon and the Sorbonne in Paris. He founded the Société Nationale des Beaux-Arts (Salon de la Nationale), and exercised a certain influence over modern painters.

2. In the list here reproduced it is interesting to note that the prices indicated are those that Mme Chabrier herself had marked on a copy of the catalogue which later came into the possession of the late Francis Poulenc, as he relates in his biography of the composer. At this time there were approximately twenty-five francs to the pound.

LIST OF WORKS

I. *Operatic and Choral Works*

Date composed	Title	Libretto	First public performance
1863	*Fisch-ton-Kan* (operetta) MS. fragments	Paul Verlaine	22nd April 1941 (Salle de l'Ancien Conservatoire, Paris)
1864	*Vaucochard et Fils Ier* (operetta) MS. fragments	,, ,,	,, ,,
1867	*Jean Hunyade* (unfinished opera) MS.	Henri Fouquier	—
1877	*L'Etoile* (opéra-bouffe, 3 acts)	E. Leterrier & A. Vanloo	28th November 1877 (Bouffes-Parisiens, Paris)
1877	*Le Sabbat* (projected opéra-comique, 1 act) MS.	Armand Silvestre	—
1877–9	1. *Cocodette & Cocorico* 2. *M. et Mme Orchestre* (2 comic duets voice & orch.) MS.		—
1879	*Une Education manquée* (1-act operetta)	E. Leterrier & A. Vanloo	1st May 1879 (Cercle de la Presse, Paris)
1880	*Les Muscadins* (projected opera, 4 acts) MS. fragments	Jules Clarétie & Armand Silvestre	—

Date composed	Title	Libretto	First public performance
1884	La Sulamite (lyric scena for mezzo-soprano female chorus & orch.)	Jean Richepin	15th March 1885 (Concert Lamoureux, Paris)
1885	Gwendoline (opera, 2 acts)	Catulle Mendès	10th April 1886 (Théâtre de la Monnaie, Brussels)
1887	Le Roi malgré lui (opéra-comique, 3 acts)	Najac & Burani	18th May 1887 (Opéra-Comique, Paris)
1888	Duo (bouffe) de l'ouvreuse de l'Opéra-Comique et de l'employé du Bon Marché	(published in Le Figaro musical, April 1893; privately performed April 1888)	
1890	Ode à la musique (soprano solo, female chorus & orch.)	Edmond Rostand	22nd January 1893 (Concert Conservatoire, Paris)
1888–91	Briséïs (unfinished opera, 1 act complete)	Catulle Mendès & Ephraïm Mikhaël	8th May 1899 (Paris Opéra)

II. Orchestral Works

Date composed	Title	First public performance
1874	Lamento (unpublished)	Société Nationale 1878
1875	Larghetto (Horn & orch.)	Société des Compositeurs 1878

Date composed	Title	First public performance
1883	*España*	Concert Lamoureux, 4th November 1883
1888	*Joyeuse Marche*	Angers, 4th November 1888
	Prélude pastoral (unpublished)	Angers, 4th November 1888

Piano works arranged for orchestra by Chabrier

1885	*Habanera*	Angers, 4th November 1888
1888	*Suite pastorale*	Angers, 4th November 1888
	(Four pieces from *Pièces pittoresques*: *Idylle, Danse villageoise, Sous-bois, Scherzo-Valse*)	
1891	*Bourrée fantasque* (MS. incomplete)	—

III. Piano Works

(a) Two hands

1862	*Souvenir de Brunehaut* (Waltzes) (First published work; plates destroyed)	—
1863	*Marche des Cipayes* (Sepoys)	—
1871	*Pas redoublé* (renamed: *Cortège burlesque*)	—
1872	*Suite de valses* (Posthumous publication, 1913)	—

Date composed	Title	First public performance
1873	*Impromptu* [1]	Société Nationale, 27th January 1877 (Saint-Saëns)
1881	*Dix pièces pittoresques:*	Société Nationale,
	1. Paysage	4th November 1888
	2. Mélancolie	(Marie Poitevin)
	3. Tourbillon	
	4. Sous-bois	
	5. Mauresque	
	6. Idylle	
	7. Danse villageoise	
	8. Improvisation	
	9. Menuet pompeux (orch. by Ravel)	
	10. Scherzo-Valse	
1885	*Habanera*	
1891	*Bourrée fantasque*	7th January 1893 (Madeleine Jaeger)
1891	*Cinq pièces posthumes:*	3rd April 1897
	1. Aubade	(Ed. Risler)
	2. Ballabile	
	3. Caprice	
	4. Feuillet d'album	
	5. Ronde champêtre	
(Published 1897)	*Air de ballet*	—

(b) Four Hands and Music for Two Pianos

1883	*Trois valses romantiques* (2 pianos)	Société Nationale, 15th December 1883 (Messager & Chabrier)

[1] The *Impromptu* of 1873 (dedicated to Madame Manet) is the earliest piano work at all representative of Chabrier's characteristic and original keyboard style. Prior to that date (although two unpublished pieces, *Rêverie* (1855) and *Le Scalp* (1861) are sometimes listed) such pieces as have survived in MS. are merely boyish experiments and according to Cortot completely devoid of interest.

Date composed	Title	First public performance
1885–6	*Souvenirs de Munich*: Quadrille for piano duet (4 hands) on themes from *Tristan and Isolde*	—

IV. Songs [1]

Date composed	Title	Words by
1870	*L'Invitation au voyage* (MS. unpublished)	Baudelaire
1880	*Sommation irrespectueuse* (published 1913)	Victor Hugo
1883	*Tes yeux bleus*	Maurice Rollinat
	Credo d'amour	Armand Silvestre
1886	*Chanson pour Jeanne*	Catulle Mendès
1890	*Six mélodies:*	
	1. Villanelle des petits canards	Rosemonde Gérard
	2. Ballade des gros dindons	Edmond Rostand
	3. Pastorale des cochons roses	Edmond Rostand
	4. L'Île heureuse	Ephraïm Mikhaël
	5. Les Cigales	Rosemonde Gérard
	6. Toutes les fleurs	Edmond Rostand
(Published 1897)	*Lied*	Catulle Mendès

All the works in the above lists, except where indicated, are published by Enoch & Costallat (Paris) and Enoch & Co. London (Edwin Ashdown).

[1] Of the following, *Credo d'amour*, *Chanson pour Jeanne*, the *Six mélodies* and *Lied* are published in a one-volume collection containing in addition: *A la musique*, *España*, the *Romance* from *L'Etoile* and two numbers from *Le Roi malgré lui*: *Chanson de l'Alouette* and *Chanson Tzigane*.

Omitted from the list are nine early songs in MS. (unpublished) dating from 1862 when the composer was twenty-one.

BIBLIOGRAPHY

BOSCHOT, A. (1947). *Portraits de musiciens.*

BRUNEAU, ALFRED (1900). *Musiques d'hier et de demain.*

CALVOCORESSI, M. D. (1907). Emmanuel Chabrier. *Grande Revue,* May.

CHABRIER, ANDRÉ (1911). Selected letters. *S.I.M. Revue musicale mensuelle,* April.

CORTOT, ALFRED (1948). *La Musique française de piano.* I. *Presses Universitaires de France.*

DELAGE, ROGER (1963*a*). Chabrier. *L'Histoire de la musique,* vol. ii. *Encyclopédie de la Pléiade.*

—— (1963*b*). Emmanuel Chabrier in Germany. *The Musical Quarterly,* January.

—— (1963*c*). Correspondance inédite entre Em. Chabrier et Felix Mottl. *Revue de Musicologie,* vol. xlix, July.

—— (1963*d*). Chabrier et ses amis Impressionistes. *L'Œil,* December.

—— (1965). Chabrier: Le Roi malgré lui. *Musica,* No. 132, May.

DESAYMARD, JOSEPH (1908). *Un Artiste Auvergnat: Emmanuel Chabrier.*

—— (1934). *Emmanuel Chabrier d'après ses lettres.*

D'INDY, VINCENT (1906). *César Franck.*

FUMET, STANISLAS (1946). Chabrier: une musique française sans detours. *Contrepoints,* January. (Now extinct.)

GIRARDON, RENÉE (1945). Le 'Don Chabrier' à la Bibliothèque Nationale. *Revue de Musicologie,* nos. 75-6.

GORER, R. (1941). Emmanuel Chabrier. *Music Review,* II.

IMBERT, HUGUES (1888). *Profils de Musiciens.*

JULLIEN, ADOLPHE (1954). Chabrier. *Grove's Dictionary.*

KOECHLIN, CHARLES (1930). Pour Chabrier. *La Revue Musicale,* January.

—— (1946). Eclipse de la Mélancolie. *Contrepoints.* I., January. *Editions de Minuit.*

MARTINEAU, RENÉ (1910). *Emmanuel Chabrier.*

PETER, RENÉ (1944). *Claude Debussy.* (rev. ed.).

PINCHERLE, MARC (1939). *Musiciens peints par eux-mêmes.*

—— (1946). Vincent d'Indy et Chabrier. *Arts,* 29th November.

POULENC, FRANCIS (1961). *Emmanuel Chabrier* (ed. La Palatine).

RENOIR, JEAN (1962). *Renoir, My Father.*

REYER, ERNEST (1886). *Journal des Débats,* 18th April.

ROBERTS, W. WRIGHT (1923). Pianoforte Works of Emmanuel Chabrier. *Music and Letters,* October.

ROLAND-MANUEL (1938). *Revue de Musicologie,* May–August.

—— (1951). Emmanuel Chabrier. *Plaisir de la Musique,* vol. iii. (Broadcast Talks).

SAMAZEUILH, GUSTAVE (1947). *Musiciens de mon temps.*

SCHNEIDER, EDOUARD (1922). *Revue Hebdomadaire,* 8th April.

SÉRÉ, OCTAVE (1921). *Musiciens français d'aujourd'hui.*

SERVIÈRES, GEORGES (1912). *Emmanuel Chabrier.*

SHATTUCK, ROGER (1959). *The Banquet Years.*

STRAVINSKY, IGOR (1936). *Chronicle of My Life.*

—— (1947). *Poetics of Music,* ch. 3.

TIÉNOT, YVONNE (1965). *Chabrier: par lui-même et par ses intimes.*

SOME RECOMMENDED RECORDS

English Catalogue

DECCA—LXT 6168   Ansermet conducts: *España, Suite pastorale, Joyeuse Marche, Danse slave* and *Polonaise* from *Le Roi malgré lui.*

SXLP—20078   Overture *Gwendoline, Fête Polonaise, Bourrée fantasque, Habanera, Joyeuse Marche* (Dervaux and Soc. Conc. Cons.).

American Catalogue

3-VOX SVBX—5400   Piano works (complete) (Renée Kyriakou).

French Catalogue

ERATO—LDE—3253   *Trois valses romantiques* for two pianos.

INDEX